Experience Miracles
@Copyright Brent Phillips 2014
Printed in the U.S.A. All rights reserved under international copyright law. Contents and/or cover
may not be reproduced in whole or in any form without the express written consent of the publisher.
Experience Miracles
ISBN-13: 978-1503242890
ISBN-10: 1503242897
NeverJustExist
1415 South Voss #110-399
Houston, Texas 77057

Experience
Miracles

BRENT PHILLIPS

1415 South Voss ~ #110-399
Houston, TX 77057 ~ USA

NeverJustExist

Forward

I just finished reading *Experiencing Miracles* and I can say that it has truly bolstered my faith in our glorious God who still works miracles today. People will approach this new book by my friend Brent Phillips in two primary ways. Some will come with skepticism and critique, while others will come longing for greater faith and desperate to see the ministry of the Spirit and miracles in their life and the Church today.

Both approaches will be blessed, though their journey will be different. I know, because I myself have approached miracles from both sides. My Lord has taken me on a long journey of theological and experiential discovery of which I have been blessed to have Brent along for part of that journey. I have been with Brent to South Africa, preaching the Word, praying for the sick and oppressed, and we have seen God do miraculous things.

I have been with Brent in the midst of loss, great disappointment and suffering. But whether we are in the midst of the victory of answered prayer or in the midst of devastating loss we are to cultivate a heart that trusts in Jesus and our heavenly Father to do abundantly more than we could ever ask or imagine. Get ready to experience miracles!

Steve Woodrow
Pastor, Crossroads Church Aspen CO
Author of *Real-ational God, Why Just Believe When God Desires To Be Known*

Thank You

Thank you to my amazing family and friends who made this book possible. I am not a self-made man but a product of those who refused to give up on me. I love you.

Special thanks to Norma Jean Lutz & Karen Morvan for helping me capture my heart on paper and my friend John Magee for taking this book from paper to print!

Contents

Introduction

My wife, Daniela works very hard at a job that is fairly physical – stretching, massaging people, and teaching abdominal exercises.

When Daniela was nearly eight months pregnant with our daughter, Jordan, she had been feeling Jordi (as we came to call her) move about every single day. However, one day as she was lying on the couch resting after a long day at work, she realized that she had not felt the baby move. Nothing at all.

At first she did not mention it to me, but the enemy instantly went to work flooding her heart and mind with all kind of fears and lies. She calmed herself by thinking that after a good night's sleep, all would be well the next day.

When she awoke the next morning, the first thing on her mind was the baby. She lay very still – waiting. Typically, Jordi was always the most active first thing in the morning.

There was no movement.

Daniela went to work, but the lies of Satan gripped her tighter and tighter. The voice of the enemy constantly accused her, saying, "You've killed your baby. It's all your fault." Then horrific images accompanied the voice as she envisioned the umbilical cord wrapped around her baby's head and neck.

However, I knew nothing of this because on the outside, she appeared calm and relaxed. Finally, before we went to bed that night she casually mentioned it to me – not appearing frightened in the least.

The next day was the same. Daniela was calm on the outside, but fear overwhelmed her inside. She felt she should call the doctor, but the fear that he might confirm that the baby was dead kept her from making that call. She simply could not face that possibility.

The next day started the same way. She lay in bed hoping for the smallest movement in her tummy, which by now, in the late stages of pregnancy, was very large.

She felt nothing.

She woke me up and told me that the baby still hadn't moved. We were both now very concerned. The atmosphere in our home became very somber. Depression started its sinister erosion into Daniela's heart.

As she drove to work, a rush of righteous anger overtook her. It seemed to wash over her and strengthen her. In a loud and commanding voice she pronounced: "Satan, in Jesus' name, you take your hands off my baby. I have prayed perfect health over this baby, and I will accept nothing less!"

And within a short while, Daniela felt Jordi move for the first time in three days. Jordi was born a few weeks later – a perfectly healthy baby!

In the early days of our pregnancy, Daniela and I had heard a story about a pastor raising his almost-dead, four-year-old daughter back to life. Unknown to me at the time, a thought passed through Daniela's mind when she heard the pastor's story. She thought, *one day I'll have to contend for the life of my child.* She pondered that thought in her heart, telling no one.

After Jordi was born, Daniela felt it was time to share that thought with me. She said, "I believe that during the time when Jordi didn't move, we were indeed contending for her life."

I was then able to tell my wife the very same thing. I, too, felt that we were in a spiritual warfare for the life of our baby.

Since that time, we have been told accounts by at least three different individuals of their baby not moving. In each case, the doctors performed an emergency C-section that very same day.

We asked our doctor about the chances of a baby not moving for three days, yet living. She said it was impossible – no movement in such a late stage of pregnancy, not even in response to prodding – means that the baby is dead.

On the outside, nothing seemed out of the ordinary, but in the spiritual realm, a battle was raging. A war for Jordan's life. It was a battle that we won, not because of who we are, but because we know beyond a shadow of a doubt that we serve a miracle-working God and we called on Him. The seed we planted – trusting the life of our child to God – brought the harvest.

That's what this book is all about.

In His Image

God is the ultimate farmer. Christians, His children, are made in His image, which means we're meant to be farmers, too.

One of God's earliest promises is that seed-time and harvest are established as a perpetual cycle. "As long as the earth endures, seed-time and harvest, cold and heat, summer and winter, day and night will never cease" (Genesis 8:22).

Because we, as Christians, don't fully understand the seed-time-harvest principle, we live far beneath our potential. The law of sowing and reaping offers Christians the potential for growing disciples, growing churches and growing the Kingdom of God. The laws of sowing and reaping also provide the key – the doorway – to the manifestation of miracles.

The principle of sowing and reaping appears all around us. Every tree, shrub, flower, and tiny blade of grass was once a seed. It was God's idea and plan from the beginning of creation. "Then God said, 'Let the land produce vegetation: seed-bearing plants and trees on the land that bear fruit with seed in it, according to their various kinds.' And it was so" (Genesis 1:11).

A seed of corn is planted in a field. That planted seed, furnished with the right amount of sun, moisture, and nutrients, will then produce a stalk of corn possibly as tall as eight feet. On that stalk, there will be dozens of ears full of corn. Each ear produces an average of 800 kernels. The multiplication from one small seed of corn takes place in one season – from one spring to the following autumn. It's a miracle.

An apple tree requires years of growth to become a mature tree and produce fruit, but once it reaches maturity, it never fails to produce a new crop of apples. Year after year after year, bushels of apples are harvested every growing season – all from one small apple seed.

God's plan for seed-time and harvest not only exists in the physical realm, but also in the spiritual. We see it repeated time after time in Scripture.

Sowing and Reaping for Moses

God parted the Red Sea for the Children of Israel to walk across on dry land in order to escape Pharaoh's advancing army. However, God partnered with Moses to work the miracle.

In Exodus 4:2, God asked, "What is that in your hand?" Moses answered, "A staff."

To Moses, it was an ordinary staff that he used every day. But God wanted Moses to see that staff as a seed for miracles – not only for parting the waters but for many other miracles as well.

Sowing and Reaping for the Widow of Zarephath

God instructed the prophet, Elijah, to find a widow woman in Zarephath because Elijah's food supply had dwindled to nothing.

God said, "Go at once to Zarephath in the region of Sidon and stay there. I have directed a widow there to supply you with food" (1 Kings 17:9).

He found the widow, but she barely had any food; she and her son were nearly starving to death. So what did Elijah do? He asked her to bake him a cake.

It seemed to be a cruel request, but this hungry widow needed a seed-planting opportunity. She baked the cake for the prophet of God (her small seed) for her supply of flour and oil never dried up (her harvest).

God didn't need the small cake; He could have produced the unending supply without it. But He invited her to plant a seed. He invites all His children to be partners in the planting and reaping process.

Sowing and Reaping for Me

I am passionate about living a miracle-filled life. Some of my earliest memories are of my mother, my brother, Clint, and I believing God for miracles of daily provisions, as well as for a number of amazing healings.

As a small child I suffered from severe asthma. I know what it's like to be rushed to the hospital while gasping for air. I know the terror of that suffocating sensation when you're unable to breathe.

Then one day, my godly mother found an amazing verse in the Bible: "...but those who hope in the LORD will renew their strength. They will soar on wings like eagles; they will run and not grow weary, they will walk and not be faint" (Isaiah 40:31).

At first, this promise became her seed. She believed the promise and repeated the verse to me often. No one could have forced her to believe that Scripture, it had to be a personal choice. It became a seed that grew in her heart. She planted the seed, nurtured the seed, and watered the seed for years. Eventually it became my seed, too. I desperately longed to "run and not grow weary."

Years passed before that seed bore amazing fruit.

I'll tell you more about this amazing healing miracle later in the book, but I want you to know that I am no stranger to experiencing the miracles of sowing and reaping.

Confusion

When I trust God, He always comes through. He is ready to do exceeding, abundantly above anything we could ask or imagine (Ephesians 3:20).

As a pastor and Bible teacher, I am deeply grieved to see Christians go through life defeated, crushed, and overwhelmed because they see God as a small God who fails to live up to His promises and has no power.

The enemy, on the other hand, seems big and powerful, and some Christians see themselves as mere "grasshoppers" (Numbers 13:33). They have either forgotten, or never really knew, what the enemy can and cannot do. They don't know who God is, and what He can do – when allowed free reign.

This confusion does not describe the God I have served all my life. The miracles I have personally witnessed would fill more than this entire book.

I will tell you true stories of miracles and you will be amazed at these testimonies. More important than the stories is the underlying principle of seed-time and harvest and the truth and power behind it. You will experience miracles.

What You Will Learn

To live a victorious, miracle-filled life you will have to learn how to walk, live and operate in the seed-time-and-harvest principle every day. *Experience Miracles* will help you to:
- Discover your expectation level (i.e., your ability to expect and believe God for miracles)
- Determine if problems and adverse circumstances have lowered your expectation level
- Uncover the basis for your expectations
- Detect when your expectations become weak and shaky

- Learn how to keep your expectation level high in the face of disaster, tragedy or some perceived failure
- Encounter God in a new way

Has the excitement you once felt at being a born-again Christian diminished to the point where you're afraid to hope for a victorious life? If that describes you, then get ready to rev up your expectation. Who could imagine a farmer planting a field of grain and not expecting those seeds to germinate, take root, break through the ground, grow up, and produce a harvest?

What's that in Your Hand?

In your walk with God, you are presented with opportunities to plant seeds. You are called upon to look past the ordinary and to see the extraordinary. God wants to partner with you in using the principle of sowing and reaping.

God is a farmer and so are you. Get ready to grasp the truths about seed-time and harvest by recognizing seeds in the ordinary events of your day. God – the ultimate farmer – wants to partner with you in His miracle-working business.

CHAPTER 1

Bad Weather

A friend retired to a farm; he plowed up a huge plot of land to plant a spring garden. When the growing season began, the crop of fruits and vegetables seemed to be perfect. The plants had dark green leaves and were filled with blooms. Those blooms soon became beautiful tomatoes, squash and corn. Then one day a thunderstorm came through the valley and destroyed all the plants and the harvest.

Farmers are more dependent on weather than almost any other occupation. If the rain doesn't come at the right time and in the right amount, the crop may fail.

God is a keeper of promises and will always do as He says He will. We limit the mighty power of God with our doubt and uncertainty. Our unbelief is like a storm that interrupts the seed-time and harvest principle.

Our God is bigger than the storm and He wants to show His children His strength (2 Chronicles 16:9).

He beckons to all. His invitation is for all. Raise your expectations in your relationship with God. You're an amazing creation. The wellspring of hope, the fountain of desires, and the source of dreams to be fulfilled are inside you.

Our amazing God changed water to wine, calmed the raging seas, and fed thousands with a small lunch. Although most of us know these Bible facts, we still tend to forget that He can do miracles in our lives, too. He can change our situation, calm our inner storms with His gentle hand and supply every need.

Imagine the power and energy behind His promises. The greatest power we can imagine will seem small in comparison with the power that God wants to release within each of us. But it's up to us to believe it is possible. Never let doubt, fear, pain, hesitancy or unbelief become negative expectancy.

You have a Part to Play

God is the same today as He has always been. The same God who parted the Red Sea is the same God who wants to work miracles in your life.

God can perform any and all miracles. However, He gave you and me a part to play in the manifestation of miracles. That's why I titled this chapter, "Bad Weather." We often allow negative expectancy to destroy the seeds of belief, the tender plants of faith and the bright red fruit of the harvest.

Perhaps it had never occurred to you that there is such a thing as a negative expectancy. But how we think, how we speak and how we believe has much to do with how much freedom God has to work in our lives. In this chapter, we're going to learn exactly how that works.

As a Man Thinketh

Belief begins in our mind. What we think guides our actions. God's perspective on a person's inner thoughts is clear in Proverbs 23:7, which says "For as he thinks within himself, so he is."

In 1903, a man named James Allen took up this subject in great detail when he wrote a book entitled, *As a Man Thinketh*. This book and the concepts that James Allen put forth became the forerunner of the self-help movement. Living in economically deprived conditions in Britain, Allen worked hard to pull his family out of financial disaster. During the worst of his trials, he discovered how his thoughts affected his future. He wrote: *You are today where your thoughts have brought you; you will be tomorrow where your thoughts take you.*

Negative Expectancy

Now let's look at a crystal clear example in the Word of someone who demonstrated a type of negative expectancy. In the book of Luke we read that a young ruler of Israel approached Jesus. Notice his limited level of expectancy.

> *A certain ruler asked Him [Jesus], "Good teacher, what must I do to inherit eternal life?"*
>
> *"Why do you call me good?" Jesus answered. "No one is good – except God alone. You know the commandments: 'You shall not commit adultery, you shall not murder, you shall not steal, you shall not give false testimony, honor your father and mother'."*

"All these I have kept since I was a boy," he said.

When Jesus heard this, he said to him, "You still lack one thing. Sell everything you have and give to the poor, and you will have treasure in heaven. Then come, follow me."

When he heard this, he became very sad, because he was very wealthy. (Luke 18:18-23)

This man was filled with incredible potential but he had negative expectations of God. He was unable to see beyond his possessions. Jesus offered him the best and most lucrative path for his life but the man walked away. He missed the miracle(s).

God's plan was not for this man to be poor. On the contrary, God's plan was for him to experience an abundant life like he had never known before. His inner negative thoughts of what he might lose caused him to go away sad. He only saw lack and deprivation.

If you surrendered all your life to God, what would you expect? Do you know God well enough to trust Him fully and completely?

Jesus knew this young man was rich. Not only did He want the man to sell everything he had, He also wanted this man to use his wealth, his riches and his hard work to share with others in need. Jesus knew the fullness that could be experienced in a life that is a *giving* life. He knew this young man would experience more joy and greater riches if he took his focus off himself and cared for others.

In verse 27, Jesus makes a startling statement: "What is impossible with men is possible with God."

This wealthy ruler believed that if he gave away all his worldly possessions, his life would be over. But Jesus wanted him to expect the impossible.

Jesus' life centered on giving. He ministered to others, set people free, healed the sick, raised the dead and then ultimately gave His life.

This young ruler was a good and respectable man – probably much admired in his community. He boasted that he'd kept all the commandments. However, because of his limited and negative vision, he was unwilling to take the next step of surrender – selling all. He thought following Jesus would not compare to his life with great wealth. His negative, partial expectation caused him to miss the opportunity of a lifetime.

I want to shout out to this man, "Are you crazy? You just received a personal invitation to join forces with the Creator of the Universe. Spiritual treasures are within your reach!"

How could he have turned away? His fear of loss blinded him to the incredible blessings of God. The thought of change was too much for him. He could have experienced transformation from worldly wealth to unending spiritual treasures but he lacked the spiritual vision to see the life God had planned for him.

Limited Vision

There is another Bible example of how expectancy affects miracles, found in Matthew 25 – the Parable of the Talents. The word *talents* in this account, refers to money not "abilities" or "giftings."

In the parable, the master (a God-type) prepares to take a journey, but before he leaves, he entrusts three servants with money. The first servant receives five talents, the second receives two and the third receives one talent. The master gave each one "according to each one's abilities." The master considered all three to be trustworthy and able to handle the gifts.

The servant with five talents invested his money and doubled it. The servant with two talents did likewise. Their excitement, their eagerness, their *expectancy* was highly evident. The third servant, on the other hand, dug a hole in the ground and buried "his master's money."

When the master returned and learned of the success of the first two servants, his words were: "Well done, good and faithful servant. You have been faithful with a few things; I will put you in charge of many things. Come and share your master's happiness!" (Matthew 25: 21, 23)

When it was time for the one-talent servant to give an account, his excuses reveal his level of expectancy:

> And the one also who had received the one talent came up and said, "Master, I knew you to be a hard man, reaping where you did not sow and gathering where you scattered no seed, so I was afraid, and I went and hid your talent in the ground. See, you have what is yours." (Matthew 25:24, 25)

What a vivid picture of negative expectancy. This servant wrongly assessed his master. This loving master wanted the servant to share in the master's own happiness but instead, the servant cowered in fear – helpless and ineffective. He cut off the flow of blessings that were destined to be his.

Not only did he miss out on incalculable blessings and miracles, but also his master called him a "wicked and lazy servant." The one talent, which he chose not to value, was taken from him and given to the first servant. Why? Because the master knew the first servant's expectancy was set on a high flame.

These two examples from the Word give a strong picture of how our thoughts and attitudes affect our ability to expect a miracle, but another story is more vivid than these. In Mark 6, Jesus, along with his disciples, returned to his hometown Nazareth. He taught in the synagogue with such wisdom that the townspeople were amazed. However, notice how their negative expectancy shut them off from the flow of miracles:

"Where did this man get these things?" they asked. "What's this wisdom that has been given him? What are these remarkable miracles he is performing? Isn't this the carpenter? Isn't this Mary's son and the brother of James, Joseph, Judas and Simon? Aren't his sisters here with us?" And they took offense at him. (Mark 6:2-3)

In the town scores of people were ill, diseased, crippled and perhaps demon-possessed. Jesus was willing to heal each one, but unbelief stifled the wonders. In that place, He could do no miracles, "except lay his hands on a few sick people and heal them" (Mark 6:5).

Becoming Apathetic

We wonder how those town folks could be so unaware that Jesus was the Messiah. How could they ignore Him and fail to see what He could do? Yet we act the same way. We give up our dreams and hopes. We give up on ourselves and assume God has given up on us, too. Instead of following our heart's passion or that big dream, we deny Him.

We love reading about God's immense power in the Bible, but we become apathetic and indifferent because we don't expect that power to make a difference in our solitary life. Our casual relationship with God represses His power. We distance ourselves from God and forget that He is limitless.

Our negativity and self-doubt spill into our souls and limit our faith in God. Too often we walk away like the wealthy young ruler paralyzed with fear, or cut off God's flow of miracles like the unfaithful servant.

Our choices create a ceiling of limitation, which does not shut off God's love but seems to intercept divine aid and separate us from His close fellowship. God is never absent; rather we are disconnected from Him by our self-imposed limitations.

There is good news. Despite disappointment or loss, we can trust God again and allow the amazing, phenomenal power of God to work in our lives. It is our choice.

CHAPTER 2

Sunshine and Rain

In the early spring, the cold dreary days of winter give way to bright skies filled with sunshine and gentle rains that revitalize the earth. Trees begin budding, grass turns a deep green and flowers shine with the cheerful colors of new life. Harvest depends on God. We plant the seed and watch Him work with optimistic, confident expectation.

As we move away from discussing the limitations of negative expectancy, let's discuss the limitless possibilities released through positive expectancy. We begin at Mark 5, which tells the story of a desperate father – a synagogue leader named Jairus.

A large crowd surrounded Jesus as his boat landed on the lake's shore. Jairus pressed through the crowd, because he had a positive expectancy.

"Then one of the synagogue rulers, named Jairus, came there. Seeing Jesus, he fell at his feet and pleaded earnestly with him, 'My little daughter is dying. Please come and put your hands on her so that she will be healed and live.' So Jesus went with him" (Mark 5:23, 24). Jairus knew his dying daughter would be healed if Jesus would come to his house. Jesus agreed and began walking toward Jairus' house. Suddenly, all the action stopped because Jairus wasn't the only person in the crowd who needed a miracle that day and he wasn't the only one who was operating with a positive expectation.

A large crowd followed and pressed around him. And a woman was there who had been subject to bleeding for twelve years. She had suffered a great deal under the care of many doctors and had spent all she had, yet instead of getting better she grew worse. When she heard about Jesus, she came up behind him in the crowd and touched his cloak because she thought, "If I just touch his clothes, I will be healed." Immediately her bleeding stopped and she felt in her body that she was freed from her suffering.

At once, Jesus realized that power had gone out from him. He turned around in the crowd and asked, "Who touched my clothes?"

"You see the people crowding against you," his disciples answered, "and yet you can ask, 'Who touched me?'"

But Jesus kept looking around to see who had done it. Then the woman, knowing what had happened to her, came and fell at his feet and, trembling with fear, told him the whole truth. He said to her, "Daughter, your faith has healed you. Go in peace and be freed from your suffering" (Mark 5:24-32)

Imagine the woman's dogged determination fueled by positive expectancy as she pushed through the crowed in spite of years of disappointment with doctors. When the woman touched Jesus, she was healed. Yet, Jesus made it clear that her faith played a significant part in the healing.

Meanwhile, poor Jairus stood off to the side watching the scene unfold. I can almost feel his impatience and frantic desire for Jesus to keep moving. At that moment, a messenger arrived to announce that his little girl was dead.

I wonder what happened to Jairus' level of expectancy. Did he stomp off in a rage? Did he cave under the weight of grief? Neither one. Jesus said, "Don't be afraid; just believe." Jairus chose to believe. His faith was rewarded.

He did not let anyone follow him except Peter, James and John the brother of James. When they came to the home of the synagogue ruler, Jesus saw a commotion, with people crying and wailing loudly. He went in and said to them, "Why all this commotion and wailing? The child is not dead but asleep." But they laughed at him.

After he put them all out, he took the child's father and mother and the disciples who were with him, and went in where the child was. He took her by the hand and said to her, "Talitha koum!" (which means, "Little girl, I say to you, get up!"). Immediately the girl stood up and walked around (she was twelve years old). At this, they were completely astonished. He gave strict orders not to let anyone know about this and told them to give her something to eat. (Mark 5:37-43)

We may wonder why Jesus put everyone out of the house until we notice the doubt and mocking. He removed the limiting negative expectation to make way for the phenomenal.

The enemy wants to steal our victories and testimonies. He plants doubts and hesitations. When these emotions surround us, our environment limits the manifestation of miracles. Environment is crucial. If Jesus had to change the environment, how much more do we also need to do the same?

If you are surrounded by people who laugh at the idea of trusting God, you may need to change your environment. Be careful about opening your heart to negative, doubting people. Instead surround yourself with those who believe. These people emulate Jesus. Together you can expect more from God.

My Personal Healing

As I stated in the introduction, I suffered from severe asthma as a child. At times my condition was so bad, I could barely walk. Trips to the emergency room were a common occurrence. After several years of suffering and having to miss out on weeks of school, my mother – a great woman of faith – read an amazing Bible promise: "But those who hope in the LORD will renew their strength. They will soar on wings like eagles; they will run and not grow weary, they will walk and not be faint" (Isaiah 40:31).

As a family we stood on this promise – especially the part that says "they will run and not grow weary…" We read the verse. We quoted it. We believed it.

I believed the promise was true so I tried out for track in elementary school. I wasn't fast enough to make the team. Then I turned to swimming. In a short time, I amazed everyone with my swimming speed. We knew swimming was an awesome miracle but the promise didn't say I would swim and not grow weary, it said I would *run* and not grow weary.

After I entered high school. I entered the 1500-meter tryouts and I not only won, I set a school record – a record that would stand uncontested for 20 years. The promise was true. Our positive expectancy proved our faith and God set my feet to running.

Few things are more terrifying to a small child than having his or her breath cut off. That suffocating feeling is what asthma is like. The miracle of moving from that condition to taking deep breaths while swimming and running made a powerful impact on me.

If that had been the only miracle I experienced in my younger years, it would have been enough. It was not the only miracle. When my father put my mother, my brother and me out of the house, we had nowhere to go. I will be forever grateful that my mother did not fall victim to self-pity, despair or bitterness during those years. Instead, she set an example for us. We learned how to believe God for the most basic daily needs such as food and shelter. Miracles were part and parcel of my growing up years.

There is no other way to experience God apart from faith. "And without faith it is impossible to please God because anyone who comes to him must believe that he exists and that he rewards those who earnestly seek him" (Hebrews 11:6).

Faith, the Pre-requisite for Miracles

My wife and I took the kids to CityCentre a few years ago. We went with a group of friends and their children. We were having dinner and the children were all playing together. We kept checking on them; then suddenly Josh, my little boy, was gone. Josh, for some reason, loves to run away. I don't know why. He's very happy! Listen, thank the Lord for the Holy Spirit, otherwise we would have to get a tracker.

All the adults began running in different directions looking for Josh. Then I saw his little face looking out of the Red Mango Frozen Yogurt door and the manager's face above him. He had gone into the store, taken a cup, helped himself, and then said: "Dad will pay." The manager said, "Where's Dad?"

Josh had total faith – the faith of a child. That kind of faith is what Jesus was talking about. The faith of a child makes no logical sense. Like the woman who wanted to touch Jesus' robe. Like the centurion that said to Jesus, "Just say the word for my servant." Nothing logical about that, but he had faith like a child. It makes no logical sense that a car could turn into a transformer, but my son says, "Why not?" Why is this childlike faith so important? Because anything is possible to him who believes.

Believe that God is good and He will reward you. He will give you the dreams and desires of your heart. He will show you His way for you. In Chapter 1, we read in Mark 6 how a group of people subdued the power of Jesus to heal because they didn't believe. We do the same with our unbelief and negative expectations.

It's easy to make a religious-sounding statement such as, "God can heal." Even the most ardent skeptic could agree. Positive expectancy takes the faith further saying, "God is healing me," "I'm in the process of being healed by God," or "I'm trusting God to totally restore my health."

When I was in Aspen I didn't have any health insurance. I went dirt biking and broke my foot in two places severely. I went to the hospital and all they did was bandage me up plus charge me $1000.00. Two weeks later, my foot was in such agony. I was preaching on crutches. A doctor in Aspen scanned my foot and said, "You should consider a malpractice lawsuit against the hospital because now we have to do surgery. Eight weeks after surgery, you'll be able to walk again but you'll never be able to walk again perfectly. You'll always feel it."

My wife and I told the doctor: "God is going to heal my foot." It made no logical sense. I preached again that week on my crutches. I preached about trusting God again and everyone was like: "uh-huh, uh-huh."

The next week I thought, *What was my touching of the robe, like that woman? What is my point of contact? What is my point of faith?* I decided I was going to go dirt biking and while I was dirt biking God was going to heal my foot. No logical sense. I took my foot out of the air cast and slipped it into that dirt bike boot. I thought I would pass out from the pain.

I went dirt biking and I came back. Oh and the pain! When I took my boot off, nothing happened. Now, not only was my foot broken, I was in horrendous agony, too. But I expected in faith that God would heal me. The next day I went riding again. When I finished riding, I took my boot off and there was no pain. I jumped on my foot and there was no pain.

We went back to the doctor and he scanned my foot again. He said, "I don't know what to say, you have experienced a miracle." I didn't go back to church with crutches. I walked up to preach the next week and everybody was amazed. Anything is possible to him who believes. Will you get back up on your faith tonight saying, "God, I've been gone for so long, I've been angry and disappointed, I've stopped believing and I've been resisting. But with faith, I'll believe for the impossible." And let me just say that sometimes, you might not get the answer you're looking for straight away. If I had given up after the first night of dirt biking when nothing happened and I was in even worse agony, I wouldn't have gotten my miracle. But I persevered and went again the next night. God is looking for faith that holds on and doesn't give up. Faith that endures until the miracle is made manifest.

Positive expectancy changes passive statements into action statements. Such statements show our faith allowing and beginning the action of God.

As the awareness of God's healing process builds in my spirit, it allows my body to surrender to His will and His timing. This knowledge also enables my faith to take root and grow. Our faith is not a "hope so" faith. No longer am I bound by a position of hoping so, but have moved into knowing so. My heart is drawn toward my God and I am propelled forward on my course.

Not Scriptural To Pray For Healing?

God stands ready to fulfill His Word and His promises. This idea is new to some Christians and appalling to others. A few years ago, I preached a sermon on healing and shared some of my personal healing experiences.

Following the service, I was shocked when another pastor totally disagreed with me. He didn't believe we should pray for healing.

This pastor said, "Gather together all the scriptures that you feel will support your belief and I'll show you where you are wrong."

We argued over many scriptures. The very idea of having a debate over the Word of God caused a deep ache in my heart. I decided I would never do that again because God needs no defense. After we expressed all our opinions, we were no closer to convincing the other. I began to pray for this man, asking God to open his eyes.

Several months later, this pastor noticed a growth on his leg. At first it was small and insignificant, but it continued to grow until he was terrified. Finally one day at his wits' end, he turned to God praying, "Lord if miraculous healing is for today, let this thing fall off my leg and be as if it had never been there."

After months of growing and causing him and his family no small concern, the growth fell off and just as he had asked, it left no mark.

Do you think this man still wanted to refute the concept that God is a healing God? Do you think he now had a higher level of positive expectancy? He had seen for himself that God's Word was true. Later I was privileged to hear him preach a message entitled, "God's Will to Heal Today."

Change Your Inner Thoughts

Your innermost thoughts determine the course of your life. Whatever picture you have on the inside, you will manifest on the outside. The contents of your heart will become the story of your life. "Guard your heart above all else, for it determines the course of your life" (Proverbs 4:23).

Jesus explained about thoughts to the Pharisees, who placed great emphasis on outward appearances. "For out of the heart come evil thoughts, murder, adultery, sexual immorality, theft, false testimony, slander" (Matthew 15:19).

In the epistle to the Philippians, Paul echoes Jesus' words about the importance of thoughts: "Finally, brothers, whatever is true, whatever is noble, whatever is right, whatever is pure, whatever is lovely, whatever is admirable—if anything is excellent or praiseworthy—think about such things" (Philippians 4:8).

We are in control of our thought life. Those who live with great expectation of God's goodness will surely experience it. Does it mean that there will be no more challenges, difficulties, or tragedies? Of course not, but the theme of our life is determined by the level of expectations.

It's up to you. Will you live with negative expectations? Or will you open the door of your heart with positive expectations to give God full reign?

CHAPTER 3

Blight

Chapter 3 **Blight**

The international grain trade watches crop
world to forecast the market supply and demand
word that a crop of rice is ruined in Southeast A.
infestation, the markets react. When a corn crop deve
disease, the world responds with higher food and fuel p   ...ds of
diseases that affect crops have scary names such as blight,   .ι and stain.
Farmers work hard to keep these conditions away from the fields.

When we face difficulties, disappointments or defeats, we would
prefer that these blights not enter our life. It is disconcerting to think of the
words suffering and miracles in the same sentence. For most of us, the two
don't seem to go together. But we may be wrong. Unlike blight, our painful
situations may open the doors to miracles. Let's take a look at Scripture to
see what God has to say about the matter.

"Dear brothers and sisters, when troubles of any kind come your way,
consider it an opportunity for great joy. For you know that when your faith
is tested, your endurance has a chance to grow. So let it grow, for when your
endurance is fully developed, you will be perfect and complete, needing
nothing" (James 1:2-4).

Some Christians sincerely believe that when bad things happen, it
is God's discipline. Because they have a deep desire to please God, they
muddle through the problems, often losing the battle, all the while thinking
they are cooperating with and working alongside God.

They say, "What doesn't kill you makes you stronger."

"Everything's going to work out for the best."

"God's just trying to teach me something through this."

Gritting their teeth, they try to apply the above verse from James to
the difficulties that face them.

We all endure loss, tragedy and suffering. But going through such
trials doesn't guarantee that we will emerge better. Many people emerge
worse. I've seen people go through a devastating loss and end up spiritually
destroyed. In the process, they become bitter, angry and resentful. Forever
scarred and living a life of total defeat. Trials and hardships are not the
source for a better life.

Suffering has a role in miracles. In this chapter we'll take a closer look

...ring and how it affects the manifestation of miracles.

Your Perception of God

What is your perception of God? Do you see Him with a big club waiting for you to mess up? Do you think He delights when you are pummeled by adverse circumstances? Some Christians say, "Why did God do that to me?" or "Why is God so mad at me?" They do not comprehend God as a loving Heavenly father.

When a couple has a new baby, they dote to the extreme. That baby never lacks for anything – food, shelter, clothing, attention or love. Jesus used parenting as an example to describe how God loves His children. "If you, then, though you are evil, know how to give good gifts to your children, how much more will your Father in heaven give good gifts to those who ask him!" (Matthew 7:11).

I may not be a perfect father, but I dearly love my children. I would never dream of causing horrendous circumstances to come into their lives. Neither does your Heavenly Father. And how much more a better Father he is than I am! Jesus said it perfectly in John 10:10, "The thief comes only to steal and kill and destroy; I have come that they may have life and have it to the full."

Life to the full. That's a huge promise.

We can navigate our way through the obstacles, suffering, troubles, tragedies and heartaches and emerge whole and victorious. It is not only possible; God has designed a way for you to be victorious through every trial. Read that again, every trial.

Joy in the Midst of Suffering

We may ask why our lives are filled with trouble and heartache and whether we can experience joy in the middle of our pain. Understanding the role of suffering in the miraculous may help us answer these questions. No one suffered like Jesus. With Jesus as our example, we can begin to see suffering as a stepping stone to a higher level of victory. The following verses summarize Jesus' attitude in the face of suffering:

Slaves, submit yourselves to your masters with all respect, not only to those who are good and considerate but also to those who are harsh. For it is commendable if a man bears up under the pain of unjust suffering because he is conscious of God. But how is it to your credit if you receive a beating for doing wrong and endure it? But if you suffer for doing good and you endure it, this is commendable before God. To this you were called, because Christ suffered for you, leaving you an example that you should follow in his steps.

"He committed no sin, and no deceit was found in his mouth."

When they hurled their insults at him, he did not retaliate; when he suffered, he made no threats. Instead, he entrusted himself to him who judges justly. He himself bore our sins in his body on the tree, so that we might die to sins and live for righteousness; by his wounds you have been healed. For you were like sheep going astray, but now you have returned to the Shepherd and Overseer of your souls. (1 Peter 2:18-25)

When the Bible says have joy in trials and persecutions, it does not mean we have joy for the suffering, but rather we can have joy in spite of the suffering, and joy for what comes out of the suffering. There's a huge difference. Jesus didn't come to earth to suffer. He came to liberate the entire planet. Suffering was the pathway to his victory.

Another scripture from Peter explains, "Praise be to the God and Father of our Lord Jesus Christ! In his great mercy he has given us new birth into a living hope through the resurrection of Jesus Christ from the dead, and into an inheritance that can never perish, spoil or fade ... kept in heaven for you, who through faith are shielded by God's power until the coming of the salvation that is ready to be revealed in the last time. In all this you greatly rejoice, though now for a little while you may have had to suffer grief in all kinds of trials. These have come so that the proven genuineness of your faith – of greater worth than gold, which perishes even though refined by fire – may result in praise, glory and honor when Jesus Christ is revealed." (1 Peter 1:3-7)

The testing of our faith produces something. When we come through the fires of difficulty and we have faith that God has everything under control, we emerge as pure gold. We emerge stronger than when we went in.

The Fiery Trial

When I lived in Aspen, Colorado, I went through a frightening fiery trial. My brother, Clint, and I conducted a Sunday evening service in our home church for a number of months. About twelve people attended – most were my family members.

One day, our pastor invited me to preach on a Sunday morning. It was a great honor that he would allow me to address the main congregation, which was usually around 250 people. Clint and I prayed that this opportunity would help build attendance for our Sunday evening service.

I owned a computer company at the time and prior to this particular Sunday, a high profile client in the area hired me as a consultant. This client managed a billion-dollar hedge fund and he was sure his computer systems were being hacked. He employed me to check out the guilt or innocence of a certain suspect. If he was guilty, he would serve time in prison due to SEC rulings.

This job was an incredible opportunity. I would earn more than I normally would have earned for such a project and I was praising God. I even got to wear a suit, which I never wore in Aspen. I did a full audit and discovered that the suspect was totally innocent. I felt great since I was able to save this man from possible prosecution.

When I presented this wonderful news to my client, I received the shock of my life. He said, "Well, that's a real problem, because we're going to meet with the FBI now."

I didn't understand.

The man added, "Unless you say that he's guilty, I am going to name you as an accomplice."

Surely not. That could never happen. Not if I told the truth, which I did.

So on that Sunday, I spoke about our amazing God and how He wants to do incredible things for each of us.

The next day, the front page of the Aspen newspaper carried a blaring headline, *Aspen Computer Solutions Owner Hacks Billionaire*. That headline was about me! The next day someone who had been in our congregation on that Sunday wrote in to the newspaper, "Get that hypocrite off the stage. We are so sick of people like him."

I did the only manly thing I knew to do. I sat at my kitchen table and cried. I cried my eyes out. I don't remember ever being so devastated or so hurt.

Clint and I had totally committed to this church. We never took a penny in pay; we had our own businesses specifically so we could give our services to the church. And then someone I didn't even know called me a *hypocrite*. I suffered for the Word's sake because I had acted according to the Word.

Defining Moment

But then a defining moment changed my attitude. I stopped whining and complaining and began to stand on God's promises. I dared to believe that this would not be the end of the road for me. I dared to believe that God was going to use this misery to do something amazing. I prayed asking God to step in, turn it around and use it as a stepping-stone. I declared God's promises aloud, confident that the devil would soon wish he'd never attacked me. We started to rejoice as if it was over long before it was over, because praise is powerful and can unlock the power of God (2 Chronicles 20:21, 22).

One of the leading businessmen in our church gave me the best advice he knew to give. He said, "Pack up and go back to South Africa because you don't stand a chance."

Truthfully, in the natural, he was absolutely right. I didn't have a chance. I didn't have the finances; I didn't have the resources; I didn't have the intelligence to fight this. But the one thing that everyone underestimated is the power of mighty God.

If God is for you, who can be against you? (Romans 8:31).

Manifested Miracles

One of the first victories we experienced was growth in our Sunday night service – people wanted to see this preacher who allegedly moonlighted as a hacker. I just kept on preaching about the goodness of God.

One day it happened. They dropped the case. The newspaper described it as *A Modern-Day David and Goliath Story*. That was the perfect analogy, because in the natural I had no chance, but because I totally trusted my Heavenly Father and because I knew He has great plans for my life, I was able to rest in the middle of the raging storm. And I did come forth as pure gold. Those in our church saw it happen from beginning to end, and their faith was bolstered.

There is so much pain and hurt and suffering going on in this fallen world. What the world needs to see is that there is hope. They can look at us and see the faithfulness and the goodness of God.

Friends of faith

"If one person falls, the other can reach out and help. But someone who falls alone is in real trouble" (Ecclesiastes 4:10).

The advice we receive in the midst of trials, challenges and tragedy can be the difference between getting up again or remaining on the mat, the difference between finishing the race and giving up.

My very first 1500m race in high school may have been the most exhausting race of my life. I had never run that far, I had never run that fast and I had never thought about quitting as many times as I did during that race. The bell rang, it was the last lap but the sound of the crowd cheering was being drowned out by the pain coming from my legs, my arms and the rest of my body. My mind started to shout "slow down", "quit!" but then I heard another voice. It was my brother. He was running in his full school uniform on the inside of the track shouting "come on my bro, you can do this! You are going to win!" His voice began to drown out the voice of pain, the voice of surrender, and he paced me right to the finish line where I broke a school record that had stood for 20 years.

One of Moses' greatest challenges, when the Israelites were trying to enter Canaan, was keeping his hands raised while the battle raged below. As long as Moses kept his hands raised, the Israelites would win, and if he did not the Israelites would lose. At first Moses stood strong but then his strength started to give way. Thank God he wasn't alone. His brother began to run that race with him, he began to help him to keep his hands raised.

Who do you have in your life when you faith is tiring? Who do you have that can lift you up again? Who do you have that when you call they won't amplify your problems but amplify your God? Who do you have who will run with you, shouting "come on, you can do it?"

How do we find this type of friends? By being this type of person. What you sow, you will reap. As you are lifting the hands of others, God is lifting your head. As you are shouting to others to keep running, you are running too.

I want you to know that you are never alone. Even if there is no one around to help you, there is a person who sticks closer than a brother (Proverbs 18:24). In our weakness He is our strength. Every time you open your Bible He is calling to you, edging you on to be the victor He made you to be. Every time you pray He is shouting to you, filling you with hope.

As Armored Tanks

Earlier in the chapter, I mentioned that some people believe they are singled out to be God's punching bag. That perception is exactly what the enemy wants you to think. In that case he would be given more free reign. But the verse from James instructs us to resist the enemy. "Submit yourselves, then, to God. Resist the devil and he will flee from you" (James 4:7).

My tactic is to change the analogy from a punching bag to an armored tank. We aren't put on earth to be knocked around but to win amazing victories. We may be navigating dangerous territory with mortars and enemy fire exploding all around us but we just keep moving forward.

A punching bag has no choice but to take a beating. A tank has power, mobility and endurance. It is on the offense at all times. In the same way we have been empowered by God to press in, to move forward, and to take ground. "Do not be overcome by evil, but overcome evil with good" (Romans 12:21).

This enabling means we are all overcomers in this world. It is a mistake to think that evil is too powerful.

Joseph's Example

Joseph is a fantastic example of pressing through in the face of great suffering. His story is found in Genesis 37-47. He started strong and ended strong.

Joseph was the favorite son of his father and hated by his older brothers. They despised him so much that they conspired to sell him into slavery and he was carried off to the land of Egypt.

Rather than complain, he maintained a good attitude and soon became great in the household of his Egyptian master, Potiphar. Even in this uncommon success, he was never proud. When Potiphar's wife wrongly accused him of attempted rape, Joseph landed in prison.

In spite of this intense suffering, he refused to allow bitterness to take root. While in prison he rose to be in charge of the entire prison system. After many years, because of his God-given ability to interpret dreams, he was promoted from prison to the position of prime minister in a single day.

Eventually, in his position as ruler, he saved the lives of his entire family. He changed the course of history.

No matter what happened to Joseph, in the prosperous times and the lean, in the times of honor and dishonor, he never wavered in his confidence that God had everything under control. He was persistent in his faith no matter what happened.

In our eyes, suffering seems so senseless, but God not only has everything under control, He also has a perfect time schedule.

The picture that God sees from His eternal, heavenly perspective is always much larger than the picture that we see from our earthly perception. "For as the heavens are higher than the earth, so are my ways higher than your ways, and my thoughts than your thoughts" (Isaiah 55:9).

Missing Miracles?

David freed a nation from war when he took down Goliath. Nehemiah restored a city when he built the wall. Esther saved a nation. Daniel came safely out of the lions' den. But the Bible says we are greater than all of them because of Jesus Christ who lives in us. So the question is: what are we doing with the Gospel that has been given to us? Are we missing incredible miracles because we've allowed suffering to become a distraction? If so, it may be time to look at the subject of suffering in an entirely new light – through the light of His perfect love.

CHAPTER 4

Love in the Garden

A good gardener loves his plants. He prepares nutrient rich soil and plants a seed at the right season and waters it faithfully. He watches for signs of infestation or disease and takes appropriate steps when one of these troubles arise. Some gardeners talk and sing to their plants. All gardeners love to see the plants grow and develop. When spring comes, these devoted gardeners fill their gardens with love.

A verse about love in the New Testament is often misunderstood: "For in Christ Jesus neither circumcision nor uncircumcision has any value. The only thing that counts is faith expressing itself through love" (Galatians 5:6).

The King James Version uses the phrase, *"faith which works by love."* It's misinterpreted when those reading it think that they will not have enough faith to see miracles because their love is inconsistent and insufficient.

While Jesus walked on this earth, He had compassion for people and because of His compassion, miracles happened. So it's certainly not wrong to think that we must have love and compassion as we're praying for others; however, that's only part of what this verse means.

God's love for me activates my faith. Ah, now that is a refreshing new perspective. When I understand how much God loves me, my faith goes into operation. I need to understand how much God loves me because faith works through love.

When we think that faith depends upon our level of love and compassion, we can slide into condemnation because we fail. The key to increasing my love for others is to increase my knowledge of how much God loves me.

Human love is inconsistent. God's love, on the other hand, is perfectly unfailing. You can count on His love. Big difference. If I am unsure of God's love for me, then doubt enters my prayers. My mind asks, *why? Why should He? Why must He? Why would God bother to answer my prayer?*

When I'm resting in His love and I'm confident of His love, then I know my prayers will be answered. It's not because I prayed it a certain way and it's not because I stated with correct articulation. It's because I asked and He is my Daddy-God who loves me. Knowing His love stimulates my faith.

If a lady whom I'd never met came into our church for the first time, and I said, "Hello, I would very much like you to bake me a chocolate cake tomorrow. Could you bring it to the church right after lunchtime?" I have absolutely no faith that I'm going to get that cake. Unless the lady has a great sense of humor.

But if I let my wife know that I have a great craving for her chocolate cake, I have much more faith that I could be eating chocolate cake by this time tomorrow. I have faith because I know the strength of our relationship and I know that love exists between us. And that knowledge triggers my faith.

Once you know and understand that your faith is activated by God's love for you, it takes all the stress and pressure out of your prayer life. When I pray for someone, I know that His love is flowing through me to that person. Now I'm basing the prayer on God's love and nothing else.

Revisit the Rich Young Ruler

Let's revisit the account of the rich young ruler found in Luke 18. We touched on the story of this man and his level of negative expectation in Chapter 1. He had approached Jesus to ask a simple, but profound question: A certain ruler asked Him [Jesus], "Good teacher, what must I do to inherit eternal life?"

Already we can admire this young man because he is a seeker. Evidently he heard Jesus teaching about eternal life and now he wants to know more. This is when Jesus began to outline the commandments but as soon as He does, the young man assures Jesus that he has kept them all. Then we come to the important moment:

"When Jesus heard this, he said to him, 'You still lack one thing. Sell everything you have and give to the poor, and you will have treasure in heaven. Then come, follow me.'

"When he heard this, he became very sad, because he was very wealthy." (Luke 18:22-23)

Which of the commandment was this man breaking? The very first one, which is, "You shall have no other gods before me" (Exodus 20:3). What was his god? His money.

As the story unfolds we can see he is a self-righteous man whose righteousness is based on his works. So with one request, Jesus demonstrates how worthless his righteousness is.

Every time we come to God with pride in how good we are, we will walk away disappointed and discouraged. It's at that point we learn how really not good we are.

Sometimes we hear a powerful message and we make vows:

"I am for sure going to do that."

"I'm serving God every day for the rest of my entire life."

"I'm giving my all for God now."

"I'm going to pray every day and fast every week."

It's all about me, me, me. What I'm going to do. A week later we're splattered on the windscreen of life. The problems come when we base our actions on what we are going to do. Such attempts will get us no further than this rich young ruler.

Why was Jesus so harsh with him? This is because he came to Jesus on the basis of the law. Jesus revealed how much of the law he *wasn't* keeping – a terribly embarrassing moment for this prideful young man.

Reason for the Law

Do you know why the law was given? To expose sin. The law illustrates how impossible it is to live perfectly. Because of the law, we know that we need a Savior. Every person on this earth needs a Savior, no one individual can live a righteous life. Only Jesus could do that and that's why we need His righteousness.

I do not come to God based on how good I am. I do not come to God based on the commandments I'm keeping. I come to God based on his mercy, His grace and His love.

The young ruler came looking for eternal life and left disappointed because his faith was based on his own perceived *goodness*. In contrast, we find accounts in the Bible of those who did not try to base their faith on themselves, how good they were, or how they kept the letter of the law. Instead they based their faith on God's mercy alone.

Trusting God's Mercy

In Matthew 15, we find the amazing account of the Canaanite woman:

Leaving that place, Jesus withdrew to the region of Tyre and Sidon. A Canaanite woman from that vicinity came to him, crying out, "Lord, Son of David, have mercy on me! My daughter is suffering terribly from demon-possession."

Jesus did not answer a word. So his disciples came to him and urged him, "Send her away, for she keeps crying out after us."

He answered, "I was sent only to the lost sheep of Israel."

The woman came and knelt before him. "Lord, help me!" she said.

He replied, "It is not right to take the children's bread and toss it to their dogs."

"Yes Lord" she said, "but even the dogs eat the crumbs that fall from their master's table."

Then Jesus answered, "Woman, you have great faith! Your request is granted." And her daughter was healed from that very hour. (Matthew 15: 21-28)

What did this woman know about Jesus? She was following after him, but why? She must have known something about His character because she begs for mercy. No one cries out for mercy from one who is unmerciful.

No doubt she had heard what He had done throughout the land. She had seen him pour out His love on others. She had heard about the healings and about people being set free. So she did not approach him based on her own goodness. She made no claims at being righteous. Even when Jesus referred to her as a *dog,* she was unaffected. She was determined to receive the miracle that she needed for her daughter based solely on the character of Jesus. And the result was a miracle – her daughter's healing.

Her faith was based on Jesus who was kind, loving and merciful. Those traits gave her the faith to trust that her daughter could be healed.

The reason we have not seen miracles in our lives is that we put faith in ourselves, in our own abilities and in our own goodness. We have faith in our faith.

Another Example of God's Mercy

Another vivid example is the story of blind Bartimaeus found in Mark 10. Look at verses 46 through 48:

Then they came to Jericho. As Jesus and his disciples, together with a large crowd, were leaving the city, a blind man, Bartimaeus (that is, the Son of Timaeus), was sitting by the roadside begging. When he heard that it was Jesus of Nazareth, he began to shout, "Jesus, Son of David, have mercy on me!"

Many rebuked him and told him to be quiet, but he shouted all the more, "Son of David, have mercy on me!"

Mercy. A person seeking mercy does not approach one who is unmerciful. This blind man called out when he heard that Jesus was coming his way because Jesus was the man of mercy. Jesus gave sight to the blind, made cripples walk and raised the dead. Jesus cared, loved and "set captives free."

Jesus is still the same today – only now He is at the right hand of God interceding for us, serving as our mediator and extending His love and mercy to us.

We don't know much about the blind man but it appears no one respected him. In verse 48 the people around him told him to be quiet. If you speak out and everyone tells you to be quiet, there's a good chance they have no respect for you. He had probably experienced very little mercy in his entire life.

Bartimaeus was essentially a pest, a bother on the lowest rung on the ladder of life. In those days you didn't get a lot of points for being a blind beggar. You were a drain on society, irritating everybody who walked past you. Except for Jesus. Bartimaeus had value to Jesus.

Jesus stopped and said, "Call him."

So they called to the blind man, "Cheer up! On your feet! He's calling you." Throwing his cloak aside, he jumped to his feet and came to Jesus.

"What do you want me to do for you?" Jesus asked him.

(Mark 10: 49-51)

You have to love those words: "Call him." The God of the universe calls for this nobody, this castoff. Surely those in the crowd were shocked.

Does it seem strange to you that Jesus would ask him what he wanted? Of course Jesus knew he was blind and needed to see but by asking the question Jesus put it in Bartimaeus' hands. To speak the end result of what he wanted.

> *The blind man said, "Rabbi, I want to see."*
>
> *"Go," said Jesus, "your faith has healed you." Immediately he received his sight and followed Jesus along the road.* (Mark 10: 51, 52)

The man, who had nothing within himself to fall back on, called on God's mercy and he received his sight. The miracle came from the perfect love of God and not of this man's righteousness or abilities.

Faith works by love – *God's* love (Galatians 5:6). The more you embrace and experience the love of God, the more miracles will be released in your life. The more miracles you experience, the bolder you will become to pray for others around you.

Now that we understand how it's God's love that authors miracles, in Chapter 5 we'll learn how our positioning plays a part in opening our lives to miracles.

CHAPTER 5

Where to Plant

Once I preached on Hebrews 4:12 about the power of God's Word. A man contacted me later. He and his wife had attended the service where I had preached. He said, "As you read verse 12, the Lord spoke clearly to me about verse 10."

The verse is about the God-kind of rest that God offers. The verse set off fireworks in his heart as he read the passage. It was such a moving experience that he had to call and tell me all about it.

Why and how did that moment come to be for this man? Because he had positioned himself. He made the decision to be in church. The subject I preached on didn't count nor did it matter if my message was good or not. What mattered was that he put himself in a place where he could hear from God; where he could receive from God. He positioned himself and it happened.

Since God is always present and never leaves us nor forsakes us, why is positioning important? Yes God is consistent. He never changes. He is always there. But we, on the other hand, can stray from His presence. Our inner spirit man can become dull of hearing and less-than-receptive to God.

The number one way to position ourselves for a miracle is to go where we know God is. Where is God most accessible to us? One place might be in a regular quiet prayer time in your own home. You open your heart and mind and pray, "Lord, I'm going to give you this time. I'm going to be quiet before you. I'm going to pray, read Your Word and listen to Your voice." Prayer and quiet time create an opportunity for God's presence.

Living in a state of expectation is another way to position yourself. Remember the phrase made popular by Oral Roberts: *Expect a Miracle.* Always be ready to receive the good and the exciting from the hand of God.

A thankful heart is a third way to position for miracles. The more thankful we are – acknowledging His provisions in our lives – the closer we come to dwelling in His presence.

Compassionate Miracle Maker

We find an account of positioning in John 5. A paralyzed man had been seeking healing for many years.

> *After these things there was a feast of the Jews, and Jesus went up to Jerusalem. Now there is in Jerusalem by the sheep gate a pool, which is called in Hebrew Bethesda, having five porticoes. In these lay a multitude of those who were sick, blind, lame, and withered, [waiting for the moving of the waters; for an angel of the Lord went down at certain seasons into the pool and stirred up the water; whoever then first, after the stirring up of the water, stepped in was made well from whatever disease with which he was afflicted.]A man was there who had been ill for thirty-eight years.* (John 5:1-6)

If we were to read Jesus' resume, one of the descriptions might be: *Compassionate Miracle Maker.* Jesus arrived in Jerusalem to attend a feast – a celebration and party with merry-making – but before the fun, Jesus went to the place in town where the needy, poor, hurting, broken, sick and diseased people were gathered. Because He had a heart of compassion. And God's heart, too. In John 14:9 Jesus said, "When you see me, you see the Father-God." He also assured us that He could do nothing of Himself, but rather does what He sees His Father do (John 5:19). So on this feast day Jesus, led by the Father, stopped along the way for a real feast. God always goes directly to the blind, the lame, the paralyzed and the hurting. His heart is full of compassion.

Years of Suffering

The man in John 5:5 suffered from his condition for thirty-eight years. A very long time. The saying "time heals all wounds" isn't true. I know a person who was deeply wounded by his father when he was five-years-old. Now at 55, he's still hurting. Time does not heal all wounds but God does. All wounds. This paralytic man has suffered for thirty-eight years, but time did not heal his condition.

In the natural, this situation looks impossible, but we serve the God of the impossible. When you face a challenge that seems to have no solution, God will step in and say, "Excuse me. Did you say impossible? That's fantastic. I've got a whole box of possible right here."

At Christmastime, Santa may show up with presents, but during turmoil-time, God will show up with miracles.

We don't know how this man became paralyzed, but we do know that he has a measure of hope and expectation, because he was at the place where he had heard that miracles happen. He was there. Each day someone helped him get to the pool. I wonder why he didn't give up and say, *"Don't come and get me today, guys. This isn't working. I'm tired of trying. I'm tired of living in disappointment and despair day after day. I give up. I quit. It's not worth the bother."* Nor did he look around and see how many other people were around the pool expecting a miracle. He didn't calculate his slim chances.

Somehow his faith has remained strong. He's full of hope. Today might be the day.

Giving Up

Too often when a person has an affliction and has been prayed for dozens of time, the manifested miracle still eludes them, so they give up. Sooner or later, someone will convince the person that it's God's will for him or her to go through this physical suffering. Someone will say, "God wants to teach you something by giving you this illness." Or, "God may be the Healer, but that doesn't mean it's His will for everyone to be healed." The longer he or she waits for the miracle, the weaker faith becomes.

How much disappointment are you willing to walk through on your way to a miracle? How many times will you ask God before you stop praying, throw up your hands in disappointment and say, "This is just the way it is. This is my lot in life. I have to learn to accept it."

The paralyzed man didn't give up. Thirty-eight years and where do we find him? We find him in the exact same place. He is one tough dude. Though paralyzed, he found a way to get to the place of miracles.

No Excuses

When my brother and I were little, there was no mercy from our mother when it came to going to church. No excuses!

"Mom, I'm too sick to go to church."

"You've got to go to church, Church is God's hospital."

"No, but I'm really sick."

"Then we really need to go to God's hospital."

I praise the Lord for her persistence and commitment. Not to say God can't heal you at home; of course He can. But when people gather together to praise God's name in corporate worship, God shows up. I want to be there when He shows up. When I least feel like being at church is the very time I need to be there.

Attending church is only one part of the equation. When we arrive with an expectant, excited heart, it won't matter if the four-year-olds are putting on a play or a speaker is boring, you will leave with something from God. Nobody comes to God and leaves empty-handed. Our Lord is not a withholder. We may show up empty-handed, but He is full and running over.

When we position ourselves correctly, His miracles flow. He created the sun, the moon, the earth, planets and galaxies with His Word. When you expect Him to speak, He will. The same God who breathed the sun out of his mouth, speaks truth into your life. He can and He wants to. Because He loves you.

An Amazing Question

The paralyzed man at the pool had no idea how his expected miracle was going to come to him. He was focused on the pool, on the water and on the rippling of the water. But the miracle came in a totally different way than he expected. God is not hampered if our theology is a little messed up and we differ on the interpretation of various scriptures. None of us will ever have perfect theology. God is bigger than our theology. He observes our faith.

This man had been paralyzed for thirty-eight years and he came to the Pool of Bethesda because he expected a miracle. On this particular day, Jesus asked him an amazing question: When Jesus saw him lying there and learned that he had been in this condition for a long time, he asked him, "Do you want to get well?" (John 5:6).

My first thought is, *Well, duh. Isn't it rather obvious?* The man is paralyzed. He's in a place where afflicted people gather to get healed. What else would he want?

But Jesus knew that not every afflicted person wants to get well. As strange as that may sound, it's true. Healing eliminates excuses for staying where you are. The affliction becomes second nature – comfortable – a part of who you are.

Sadly, we find safety in our problems and hurts. We wouldn't know what to do if we didn't hate anymore or if we forgave someone. If we constantly talk about our problems and God took those problems away, what would we have to talk about?

It seems crazy, but not everyone wants to be healed, be delivered, or set free. That's why Jesus asked.

This man could have answered Jesus by saying, "I don't believe I can get healed," but that was not his perspective. Instead, he replied, I have no one to help me into the pool when the water is stirred. While I am trying to get in, someone else goes down ahead of me (John 5:6).

All We Need is Jesus

After all these years, the man is confident that if he can just get into the water, he will be healed. He is still full of expectation and faith. Oh that we would all have such tenacity and determination. He's close to receiving his miracle. Now Jesus is ready to show him that he need not depend on other people to have his needs met – all he needs is Jesus.

Our world runs here and there seeking answers to their problems and provision for their needs – everywhere except at the feet of Jesus.

When Jesus visited the home of the sisters, Mary and Martha, He found Martha in a tizzy trying to get dinner on for all the guests in her home. She longed to please this group with her culinary skills and her great hospitality. But she was seeking approval in the wrong way. "Martha, Martha," the Lord answered, "you are worried and upset about many things, but only one thing is needed. Mary has chosen what is better, and it will not be taken away from her" (Luke 10:41).

When we look to people rather than God, we are bound to be disappointed. Jesus didn't address the idea that the paralyzed man thought he needed someone else to help him. Instead, in verse 11, He told him to get up, pick up his mat and walk.

This man had not used his legs for almost forty years. Now Jesus is commanding him to get up and walk. Can you imagine the faith that it took for him to actually begin to move – to rise from his prone position and stand? But he believed Jesus, he obeyed and he was immediately healed.

Positioning for Miracles

Positioning is crucial if we are to receive miracles. This man's effort to be in the right place at the right time positioned him to receive the healing.

It's up to each one of us to position ourselves physically, mentally and spiritually to be in the place where God dwells. It's up to us to remain always in a state of excited expectancy.

In the next chapter, we find that while God provides the miracles, seed-planting is up to us.

CHAPTER 6

Seed

Seeds are found in every plant. A peach has one large seed. A strawberry has hundreds of seeds all over the fruit. The acorn falls from the mighty oak to sprout into a new tree. Seeds are everywhere. A farmer or gardener cares for the seeds, keeping them dry and safe. Then when the time is right, the seed is placed into the ground to germinate and reproduce. Sowing and reaping are the stepping stones to experiencing God's miracles. God instigated the principle of seed-time and harvest in Genesis. "As long as the earth endures, seed-time and harvest, cold and heat, summer and winter, day and night will never cease" (Genesis 8:22).

The Word of God – the Bible – is the seed that brings miracles. Let's examine a basic biblical precept about the Word.

"All Scripture is God-breathed and is useful for teaching, rebuking, correcting and training in righteousness, so that the servant of God may be thoroughly equipped for every good work" (2 Timothy 3:16,17).

The Word of God, the Bible, is *God-breathed*. Every time I read the Word, I am in some way experiencing God's presence – His breath. The Bible is designed to be life changing and to equip Christians for *every* good work.

When we are born into this world, we arrive with missing pieces in our emotions and our minds. As we move through life, adverse circumstances knock out more and more pieces until we become fragmented.

Before my mother came out of an abusive marriage situation and got a divorce, she suffered many hurt-filled and broken years. Yet, she became whole and complete. One day while searching God's Word, she read the verse in Joel in which God promised to "restore to you the years that the swarming locust has eaten" (Joel 2:25 NKJV). God breathed that guarantee into her inner spirit. It became her personal promise.

Today, she reaps the harvest of that Word-seed because she is restored and whole (complete) in her emotions and in her spirit. She is thoroughly equipped to do the works God calls her to do. No Christian can carry out what God has designed us to do without a solid foundation of planting the Word into our spirits.

In Matthew 4:4 Jesus clearly states, "Man shall not live by bread alone, but by every word that comes from the mouth of God."

In biblical times, bread was the staple diet. Today, we could rephrase the verse: "We cannot exist on physical food alone. We must have God's Word in order to flourish and grow." Imagine what it would be like to eat one meal a week. Our bodies would quickly become weak and emaciated. Many people walk around with emaciated spirits, because they are not feasting on the life-giving, God-breathed, Word of God on a regular basis. The Christian with an emaciated spirit is ineffective and powerless against the onslaught of the enemy.

We used to believe that sowing a seed would bring a harvest. I remember one day my brother had no money. On the way to church, he found 10 cents on the floor. With the faith of a child and much excitement, he put the 10 cents in the offering bowl. It wasn't even his money!

While he was at church God gave him an idea for a chocolate business. He began buying these slabs of chocolate and making these shapes for Easter. And he couldn't sell them fast enough!

Sowing a seed reaps a harvest.

As I've been writing this book, I have repented to the Lord for how far we've come, from where we used to trust him for everything.

I have not been living a life of faith. I've been living a life of reason, full of what makes sense and what's safe. When I began the Encounter God Bible Study in Houston, I knew it wasn't logical to leave where I was serving God and to go start up a new venture. But I also knew God was calling me to step out in faith. The first night, more than 800 people showed up.

The Bible says that seeds will produce after their own kind. What seeds have you allowed to be growing in the garden of your heart? I had never heard anything contrary to the message that God heals. Then when I went to Aspen, people started to share Scripture with me that seemed to say that sometimes God doesn't heal. I had never heard that before. I'd only heard that God healed. Suddenly these little doubt-seeds started to get planted in my heart.

Have you heard about Paul's thorn?

Those seeds began to grow. Where I used to believe that anything was possible, now I started to believe that some things were possible.

On that path, you will eventually start to believe that almost nothing is possible.

Ask God to take doubt from your mind. Tell him, *I want to believe in*

You for who You are because anything is possible.

Parable of the Sower

Jesus explained the importance of seed-time and harvest in the parable about the sower. The parable is found in Matthew 13 and also in Mark 4. In both accounts after speaking the parable, Jesus took the time to explain it point by point. In Mark 4:13, He makes a statement that we tend to gloss over. In fact, I've never heard this verse discussed or emphasized. When the disciples asked the exact meaning of the parable, Jesus said, "Don't you understand this parable? How then will you understand any parable?" (Verse 13)

This one parable is the grand-daddy of all parables. If you don't understand the truth of this parable, then you will never have the capacity to understand any other parable in the Bible.

We should be eager to dig deep, study the Parable of the Sower and learn all we can from it. If we miss this basic concept, we will completely miss how to activate the seed of the Word of God in our lives. Here is that parable.

Again Jesus began to teach by the lake. The crowd that gathered around him was so large that he got into a boat and sat in it out on the lake, while all the people were along the shore at the water's edge. He taught them many things by parables and in his teaching said: "Listen! A farmer went out to sow his seed. As he was scattering the seed, some fell along the path, and the birds came and ate it up. Some fell on rocky places, where it did not have much soil. It sprang up quickly, because the soil was shallow. But when the sun came up, the plants were scorched and they withered because they had no root. Other seed fell among thorns, which grew up and choked the plants, so that they did not bear grain. Still other seed fell on good soil. It came up, grew and produced a crop, multiplying thirty, sixty, or even a hundred times." Then Jesus said, "He who has ears to hear, let him hear." (Mark 4:1-9)

Jesus begins, "Listen! A farmer went out to sow his seed." God is a farmer and we are made in His image. We are the farmers (or the sowers) in this parable. The seed in this parable is the Word of God.

When you open your Bible and read the Word of God, you sow a seed into your personal life. The Holy Spirit then helps the seed to grow. You must sow into your life. If your pastor is the only sower of the Word in your life, then you are in a lot of trouble because you only hear him speak a few hours each week.

This parable makes it clear that we are all responsible for sowing the seeds of the living Word. Neglecting the act of sowing the Word can be catastrophic. Once we realize the truth behind this teaching, and realize exactly what is happening in the supernatural realm, none of us will ever want to stop sowing.

God is the Author of Sowing and Reaping

A farmer is not responsible for inventing the law of sowing and reaping. It is a spiritual concept that became an earthly concept. God created the earth and seed-time and harvest. This earthly concept is a spiritual concept to show on the earth a model of heaven. Sowing and reaping is a God concept – not an earth concept.

God put seed-time and harvest into our earth and then He said everything on earth will operate by this principle. One of the first instructions he gave Adam and Eve was to be fruitful and multiply (Genesis 1:22 and 1:28).

When you sow you will reap. It's a law as much as the seasons. People buy ski passes long before it turns cold. In warmer climates, we prepare backyard pools before the heat arrives because we are confident that the weather is going to change. When we sow the Word of God, we can be super confident that we will reap the results.

The Word of God is the seed. Peter re-emphasizes how God uses the seed principle even in our salvation. This is how He operates: "For you have been born again, not of perishable seed, but of imperishable, through the living and enduring word of God" (1 Peter 1:23).

100% Yield

God said, "Let there be light," and there was light. (Genesis 1:3) In the process of creation, God sowed a seed by speaking His Word. The yield was 100%. It's an amazing miracle and a pattern we can follow every day.

When a farmer plants seeds, maybe 80% will germinate and grow and produce. God's incorruptible seed, on the other hand, yields 100% results. Not sometimes, not maybe, but every time we activate the seed of the Word, it bears a harvest.

When we study the life of Jesus and study the healing miracles, every person that came to Jesus in faith walked away with the miracle they needed. As we learned in Chapter 1, the only times miracles don't manifest are when Jesus comes face-to-face with unbelief. Faith activates the seed of the Word. When you mix faith with the imperishable Word of God, you get a harvest.

"In the beginning was the Word, and the Word was with God, and the Word was God. He was with God in the beginning. Through him all things were made; without him nothing was made that has been made" (John 1:1-3). Jesus, the Incarnate Word, was with God from the beginning, and it was through Him that all was created. As we read the creation account in Genesis, we see, "God said…." He used the Word to create.

We believe God spoke a whale into being. We believe He spoke the oceans into existence and separated the waters so dry land appeared. But when it comes to believing that Scriptures can actually come to pass in our lives, then we get stuck.

I hear people say,

"Does God *really* mean that I can be healed?"

"Does He *really* mean that I can always triumph against the enemy?"

"Does the Word really mean that I can be free from worry and fear?"

"Will God really forgive me?"

And on the list goes. There's no confidence. No assurance. "But let him ask in faith, nothing wavering. For he that wavereth is like a wave of the sea driven with the wind and tossed" (James 1:6 KJV). If we believe that God created the universe by His Word, then why is His Word any different when we say it? If Jesus were physically standing with us today, what would be the difference between my speaking God's Word and His speaking it?

The only difference would be that Jesus is God and was always totally confident that the Word was sufficient to produce the needed results. He knew that Word would change physical conditions. He spoke and a tree withered up from the roots. His words calmed a raging storm.

The spiritual Word of God as a planted seed affects physical circumstances. Now it's time to learn about preparing the soil for the seeds to grow.

CHAPTER 7

Soil

A friend bought a house that had belonged to a family with young children. On the property was a playground. The area was partitioned off from the grass and was filled with sand. My friend thought it would be a great idea to plant a garden in this already-cleared section. She worked hard, building rows and planting seeds. However, this sandy soil was not made for growing. Few plants came up and those that did were scraggly and yellow. The few plants that lived produced tiny, knotty unappetizing vegetables.

Soil Matters

In Chapter 6, we discussed the importance of a seed and God's principle of seed-time and harvest. But growing a seed is not an automatic process. You can walk out to your back yard and throw out a handful of flower seeds, but the chances of any of the seeds germinating and growing are slim because the soil has not been prepared. Most yards are covered in thick grass, which prevents the flowers from taking root and surviving.

Jesus said that if we do not understand the Parable of the Sower we cannot understand any parable. Seed-time and harvest have certain guidelines and a definite process. Though we long for a harvest in our lives, few of us actually realize how to go about growing the seeds and reaping the harvest.

The beauty of the parables of Jesus is that they are timeless. Sowing and reaping is something that people understood two thousand years ago and we understand yet today. It's a simple concept. If he had taught physics or chemistry, perhaps not everyone would understand, but we all grasp the notion of putting a seed in the ground. Even kindergarten students can fill a styrofoam cup with dirt, add a few bean seeds and then watch with wonder as a green tip emerges from the dirt.

Different Desires

We have established that the seed in this parable is the Word of God, but how can we plant a seed of the Word and reap a harvest?

For instance, how can we take one verse that says, "By his stripes we are healed," and from that statement receive a healing in our bodies? How will we take a Scripture that says, "For God so loved the world that he gave his only son," and apply it to receive salvation?

We can find nuggets in the Word and discover God's plan and purpose for our life.

All of us have different desires. Some may want to see our family serve the Lord. Some may want to go to a deeper place with God. Some may desire to go into full-time ministry. Some may need a physical healing. Some may simply want to make a difference for God. Whatever it is, you have a desired harvest – probably more than one.

Prepare the Soil

The first step to harvest is to prepare the soil. In the parable of the seed, the only thing that changes from one example to the next is the soil. We are the soil; the condition of our heart determines if we are ready to receive the Word.

When a farmer surveys a patch of ground that has not previously been used for growing crops, he will not simply hook the planter to the tractor and begin going across the field scattering seeds. That would be a waste of time, energy and fuel, not to mention the cost of the seed. First the land must be cleared and prepared.

Four hindrances need to be removed:

- Rocks
- Weeds
- Roots
- Trees

Rocks

Rocks are the obstacles that get in our way. Rocks are not a little stone that you can just pick up and toss out of the way. Rocks are like boulders. You're going to have to get down and get dirty. You may need help with these obstacles. You may even need dynamite. As long as there are rocks in the garden, very little growth can happen.

Envy and Selfish Ambition

"For where you have envy and selfish ambition, there you find disorder and every evil practice" (James 3:16).

James points out two major boulders that need to be cleared off your land in order to be prepared for a harvest – envy and selfish ambition. Envy means that you are unable to rejoice in another person's blessings. *Why couldn't that be for me? They have all the luck. Nothing ever turns out right for me.* A heart filled with envy has very little room for seeds to grow into an abundant harvest.

Selfish ambition is pretending your motive is for the greater good yet really acting for your own personal reasons. For instance, if I were to tell everyone how much I love to preach God's Word, when in reality all I want is to be the center of attention, that would be selfish ambition.

Selfish ambition may be serving in the church in order to boss people around and be in control.

On the surface, selfish ambition appears to be a small issue, but let your plow hit a boulder and you won't plow very deep. When seeds fall upon rocks there is not enough soil to put down roots. Philippians 2:3 clearly instructs us to "Do nothing out of selfish ambition, but in humility consider others better than yourselves." We can solve many problems when we prefer others above self.

Most people at the top of organizations love to order people around. Jesus had a completely different viewpoint. Jesus came to serve. He demonstrated service as he washed the feet of His disciples. Serving others breaks the back of selfish ambition. Ask God to reveal ways to bless others. Do for others and keep silent about it. Take on the tasks that no one else wants to do. Selfless acts of mercy are the best way to conquer selfish ambition.

Pride

Pride only breeds quarrels, but wisdom is found in those who take advice (Proverbs 13:10). Pride is another obstacle that can prevent a harvest. Ask the Lord to show you areas of pride in your life. Pride prevents a person from heeding wise advice. Usually, the reason wise advice is not taken is due to pride and arrogance. The person thinks he or she knows more than the one who is giving the advice. Admitting that we don't know everything helps us see why we need a Savior and why we need the Holy Spirit – our Teacher.

"By your great skill in trading you have increased your wealth, and because of your wealth your heart has grown proud" (Ezekiel 28:5).

I have had the privilege of personally meeting some very wealthy people. One of the challenges they face is pride. Why take advice when you can buy anything you need and you can tell anybody what to do? The wealth calls all the shots. Remaining humble and receiving wise advice is difficult. Pride has a way of creeping up on us. When it does, it prevents our seeds from taking root.

Unforgiveness

Matthew 6:15 says, "But if you do not forgive men their sins, your Father will not forgive your sins." The Amplified version of this verse puts it this way: *"But if you do not forgive others their trespasses [their reckless and willful sins, leaving them, letting them go, and giving up resentment], neither will your Father forgive you your trespasses."*

Unforgiveness is a rock that is holding more people back than we imagine. A past betrayal was so devastating that now it seems right to refuse to forgive.

But unforgiveness is a chain that forever binds us to our past. The big lie of the enemy is that it "doesn't matter one way or the other." But unforgiveness stands between us and the sweet forgiveness of our Savior. What a terrible price to pay. I know how much I need God's forgiveness. So because I never want to be compromised in any way, I choose to forgive others. I keep my land cleared so that I will reap a great harvest.

The best way to clear out all the rocks and boulders is to daily ask God what they are, and where they are.

"Where am I prideful?"

"What am I doing for all the wrong reasons?"

"Where is envy and jealousy in my life?"

God is faithful to show us our rocks and faithful to help us remove them from our soil.

Weeds

Weeds are disrupters – thorns (verses 18 and 19). The Amplified version is deeply descriptive. "And the ones sown among the thorns are others who hear the Word, then the cares and anxieties of the world, the distractions of the age, the pleasure and delight, the false glamour and deceitfulness of riches and the craving and passionate desire for other things creep in and choke and suffocate the Word and it becomes fruitless."

Cares of the World

Cares, anxieties and distractions are problems for almost everyone. People who love God come to church and hear the Word, but there are weeds, which are choking out the seeds of the Word.

These distractions are many and varied but let's look at a few. Start with the daily news. People are consumed with watching or reading the news. They are upset about this and that and yet they continue to watch for hours each day.

Consider how much of a difference it makes in your life. Are you better for knowing every detail of what's going on in the world? I'm not saying we should not be aware of the happenings around us, but we must keep it in a good perspective. It's possible to switch on CNN and watch news in every single country of the world. There's a cyclone here, a flood here, a drought there, a murder there, an uprising in this or that country. If the news consumes you and you complain and are distracted, it may be that God's Word is being squeezed out of your life.

These weeds take your focus off of God. On the one hand we say, "God, I'm going to live for you. I believe you to show up big in my life. I believe you're taking me to the next level."

This is a sincere prayer to God, but at the same time we wring our hands, "This world is a terrible place. It's so hard to raise a child in this scary world. The world's a mess. The weather's a mess. The government's a mess." When we focus on these things, it's no wonder God's Word isn't affecting us.

I want to be informed, but I'm careful to keep it secondary to God's Word. I don't want to be informed at the expense of what God says.

If this has become a serious distraction between you and God's Word, between you and your fellowship with God, you may need to switch off the news. If instead you spend time sowing God's Word in your heart, your garden will begin to produce a great harvest.

Deceitfulness of Riches

Recently, I made a trip to Las Vegas. That city is all about the glamour of wealth. They offer the best hotels, the best food and the best shows. Rooms are available for tens of thousands of dollars a night with people waiting on you hand and foot. Bright lights, glitter, fancy cars, jewels, and furs. It's all there.

I arrived on Thursday and heard buzzing in the airport. Everyone was pumped and excited and expecting to make money and have an incredible time. When I made my return trip on Sunday, the airport was entirely different. People walked along with their heads down with solemn expressions – all the excitement gone. They'd been fooled by the deceitfulness of riches.

Riches deceive and cause us to become comfortable and complacent so that we no longer look to God.

Jesus gives a vivid example of this in a parable in Luke:

Someone in the crowd said to him, "Teacher, tell my brother to divide the inheritance with me."

Jesus replied, "Man, who appointed me a judge or an arbiter between you?" Then he said to them, "Watch out! Be on your guard against all kinds of greed; a man's life does not consist in the abundance of his possessions."

And he told them this parable: "The ground of a certain rich man produced a good crop. He thought to himself, 'What shall I do? I have no place to store my crops.'

"Then he said, 'This is what I'll do. I will tear down my barns and build bigger ones and there, I will store all my grain and my goods. And I'll say to myself, "You have plenty of good things laid up for many years. Take life easy, eat, drink and be merry."'

"But God said to him, 'You fool! This very night your life will be demanded from you. Then who will get what you have

prepared for yourself?'

"This is how it will be with anyone who stores up things for himself but is not rich toward God." (Luke 12:13-21)

Those who are poor wish to be rich and those who are rich become disillusioned because the money did not bring the joy and happiness that was expected. Wealth sometimes brings sorrows.

"The blessing of the LORD brings wealth and he adds no trouble to it" (Proverbs 10:22). Only God can give wealth and contentment at the same time.

Craving and Passionate Desires

The intense craving for material things becomes a prime motivator. We work hard to earn more in order to be able to buy more. It's an endless cycle. It seems normal, because everyone around us is doing the same thing. The biggest house, the largest TV screen, the latest iPhone, the nicest car and the most fashionable clothes. More, more, more seems to be the motto of people's lives. This includes the rich and the poor and those in the middle. Everyone thinks they need something else that they don't have.

The craving is subtle; we don't realize we've been sucked into the trap. It's time to recognize that when I fully trust God, He will bring to me exactly what I need at the time I need it and it will not be for the purpose of impressing others.

The desire for riches is one of the weeds that slowly squeezes God's Word and your desire for God out of your life. When you are concerned about building bigger barns like the man in the parable and you concentrate on possessions, the more the cravings diminish your eternal vision and perspective. Your desire to grow in the Lord is replaced with a desire to grow in your accumulation of possessions.

Roots

Roots hidden under the soil will hinder the planting and growing process. Roots represent obstructions. A number of years ago, while we were still living in South Africa, I talked to my mother about landscaping to make our home look better. This idea resulted in a competition. Mom gave one hundred dollars each to Clint and me to create our gardens.

My section was right outside my bedroom window. I was excited about making it come to life. I cleared out the rocks and I pulled the weeds, but then I discovered clumps of roots. In some cases, I couldn't really tell where they came from. These roots required more work than the weeds, because it took time to find the source and to dig them out.

Spiritual roots are the little problems that we let slide. We pay little attention to them. Roots can include prejudices, behavior issues and pet peeves (what gets on our nerves).

For me, it happens when I drive to work. It's not a long drive but it seems no one else on the road knows how to drive. They cut in front of me, they fail to use their turn signal, they drive under the speed limit – especially when they're right in front of me. It's enough to make me crazy. The interesting thing is, I'm all upset and that person is totally unaware. Who is messing up whose life? I've lost my joy and my peace, and I've not even arrived at my workplace yet.

Prejudice

In my travels, I have learned that every nationality believes they are the best and tends to think they are a little better than others – smarter, harder workers, tougher, more creative. This attitude results in putting others down and belittling others.

These roots have no place in our garden. Prejudice gets in the way of God's plan and purpose. For example, God may lead you to witness to a certain person, but your subconscious mind thinks they don't deserve His love. Roots get into the soil disrupting the planting and growing process.

"Therefore, since we are surrounded by such a great cloud of witnesses, let us throw off everything that hinders and the sin that so easily entangles. And let us run with perseverance the race marked out for us, fixing our eyes on Jesus, the pioneer and perfecter of faith" (Hebrews 12:1, 2b).

God tells us to throw off everything that hinders us and so easily entangles us. Roots grow from opinions and ideas that we have collected from earliest childhood. Words spoken over you, deeds done to you, adverse circumstances. You don't like this person. You don't like that person. This isn't the way you wanted it done. This dream fizzled out; those plans fell through. All through the years, you've picked up all these root starters. They weigh you down, yet you're unaware they are there.

Imagine a marathon runner dressed in multiple layers of clothing. He may finish the marathon, but will not be able to run fast, because the extra clothes hinder. Spiritually, you can function with the weights that hinder, but you can't face every situation. If someone speaks to you a certain way, you might explode in anger.

Don't think, *I've always been like this; I've always had this problem. This is the way I was raised. It's just the way I am.* These thoughts are lies from the enemy. If God's Word says we can throw off all the weights, then we can. We have much more than a marathon to run, we have a race that lasts a lifetime. We cannot move at the pace that God wants if we are laboring under heavy burdens. Ask God to show you the roots in your life that need to be removed then get busy and clear your land.

Trees

I love trees. They're beautiful. They provide shade, they provide homes for the birds and they cool the air. Trees are wonderful but one in the middle of a garden is a major problem. It's hard to run your plow and prepare the soil with a tree in the way. Also, the shaded area will not grow well and hidden roots spread out to cause problems for growth.

Spiritually, the trees are the good areas that may be unnecessary and need to be moved to the periphery. For example, certain friends who are very nice people, but will not help you to go where God leads.

You may want to plant a beautiful garden, but these friends stand in the way. These friends don't help with the plowing nor do they say, "Let me help you with this garden. Let me clear the way." Rather, they stand in the way.

It isn't necessary to cut these friends out of your life forever and never speak to them again. But they may not need to be in the center of your life at this time.

Watching TV can be problematic. TV is not inherently wrong, but if it gets in the way of your time in God's Word, it hinders the building of your faith. Ask yourself if the TV programs you watch build up your excitement for God. TV may be a tree that needs to be moved to the periphery so that your garden can flourish.

Take inventory of how you spend your time. Where does God rank in your schedule? Time spent with hobbies, computer games, hours at the gym are not wrong unless they stand in the way of the best that God has for you. Work diligently on your garden. Get your garden flourishing first and then allow time for other activities. Then you will have time to sit under the shade and enjoy the trees. "But seek first his kingdom and his righteousness, and all these things will be given to you as well" (Matthew 6:33).

Preparing the soil in order to reap a harvest requires attention, discipline and diligence. After the preparation is the time to plant and then to water those plants. We'll find out more about planting and watering in Chapter 8.

Planting and Watering

In Texas where I live, the heat of summer zaps the moisture from the soil. It seems that those plants in small pots dry up by the hour and need watering morning and night. Plants need water. If they don't get that moisture they will die.

Jesus related many more parables than are recorded in the Bible. In fact, in Matthew 13:34 we learn that *he did not say anything to them without using a parable.*

I find this idea fascinating. Jesus, the master teacher, was also the master storyteller. He created vivid allegories that painted pictures in the minds of His listeners. He talked about crops, livestock, families, neighbors, treasures and fields. Common visuals easily seen with the mind's eye. However, the deep meaning of His parables was sometimes veiled. Only those with searching hearts grasped the deeper meaning.

When He told the Parable of the Sower, the disciples wanted to know what it meant (Mark 4:10). Jesus did not turn them away. He took the time to carefully explain each point.

Satan Wants to Steal the Word-Seed

As we have looked at the Parable of the Sower, we see how it relates to miracles and we've discussed the seed and clearing the soil. The next step is to plant and water. The Bible is clear that what we plant is extremely important. "Do not be deceived: God cannot be mocked. A man reaps what he sows" (Galatians 6:7).

Planting the Word in our lives is important, but in Mark 4:17, we discover that Satan relentlessly is attempting to steal that Word as soon as it's planted. "Some people are like seed along the path, where the word is sown. As soon as they hear it, Satan comes and takes away the word that was sown in them" (Mark 4:17).

Why does Satan want to steal the Word from you? Is it because you attend church? Is it because you're a nice person? Is it because you know a few Bible verses? Is it because you sing all the right songs and know all the right Christian phrases to use?

None of the above.

Satan steals the Word because he doesn't want it to take root and grow in your life. He doesn't want the Word to be effective for you. He definitely does not want you to live by what the Word says.

Although thousands of American families own a Bible, very few dig in to read and study and learn. Simply being in possession of a Bible will do nothing to change your life.

When Bad Things Happen

We need the Word to be effective, because the enemy is prowling around looking for whomever he can devour (1 Peter 5:8). Bad things happen to people everyday. Like I have said previously, I suffered from severe asthma as a child but we did not let that adverse circumstance have the last say. My mother planted the seed of the Word. She planted it in her heart and she planted it in my heart as well. That seed grew and produced an abundant harvest of good health, freedom from asthma, and a desire to serve God.

The satanic principles that the world lives by do not bring heavenly results. Heavenly principles produce heavenly results. To plant and water God's Word is to give it entrance into your heart and mind enabling you to believe what it says and then understand what it says. "Wisdom is supreme; therefore get wisdom. Though it cost all you have, get understanding" (Proverbs 4:7).

A package of beans on the shelf of your pantry will never sprout, never grow. But plant those seeds in good soil and give it water and light, and those seeds will burst with life, producing an abundant harvest.

In the same way you can be in church every Sunday, read a Scripture each day, but that's no guarantee your faith will grow. If the Word isn't planted in good soil, if it's not getting the necessary light and water, you're no better off.

Revere and Respect the Word

We plant and water when we revere and respect God's Word. Job said, "I have not departed from the commands of his lips; I have treasured the words of his mouth more than my daily bread" (Job 23:12). Job treasured the words from God more than his physical food. If Christians were to treasure God's Word more than their food, we would see dynamic miracles taking place.

God wants us to elevate His Word. If we believe the Word is the final authority, then we will act like we believe it.

For example, if financial problems come our way, we will believe that the Lord will grant abundant prosperity (Deuteronomy 28:11).

If we are upset and agitated, we will believe the His peace will keep us (Isaiah 26:3).

If the doctor diagnoses a disease, we will believe that by His stripes we are healed. (Isaiah 53:5).

We believe that the name of Jesus is above all other names on earth and we will act accordingly. We will trust Him to be true to His promises.

Renew Your Mind

"Keep this Book of the Law always on your lips; meditate on it day and night, so that you may be careful to do everything written in it. Then you will be prosperous and successful" (Joshua 1:8).

"But his delight is in the law of the Lord, and on His law he meditates day and night. He is like a tree firmly planted by streams of water, which yields its fruit in its season and its leaf does not wither; and in whatever he does, he prospers (Psalm 1:2, 3).

These two scriptures are amazingly similar. They instruct us to meditate on the Word day and night, and then promise success if we do. In spite of this wonderful promise, this is an area where many Christians are found to be lacking. Because we live in a world filled with noisy distractions, it's not always an easy thing to meditate on the Word. Easy or not, it's a matter of victory or defeat in our ongoing war with the enemy.

Realizing that it's impossible to think of two different subjects at once, we can train our minds to concentrate on Scriptures. Personally, I do this because of a lifetime of training. When unbidden thoughts come to mind, I defeat them by turning my mind to specific Scriptures. God has given clear instructions that we not conform any longer to the pattern of this world, but we are to be transformed by the renewing of our minds (Romans 12:2). The more we concentrate and give attention to the Word, the more our minds will be renewed. Once our minds are renewed, actions will follow.

There are many ways to meditate on God's Word. Some possibilities include:

- Take time to read a verse or passage over and over.
- Begin to memorize all or part of it.
- Listen – quiet your heart to allow the Holy Spirit to speak to you through God's Word.
- Consider how it fits with the rest of the Bible and life in general.
- Become emotionally involved – allow yourself to feel what God feels, His desires expressed through his words.
- Move from meditation to application – connect your thoughts to action. Consider how the truth and power of the Word of God should affect your behavior.

Meditating on God's Word is a basic discipline of the faith just as much as prayer, Bible reading, worship, church attendance and witnessing. It is a crucial way to water the seed of the Word in your spirit.

Eyes Create an Image

It's imperative that Christians be careful about what they look at with their natural eyes. Avoid what is not pleasing to God. In our extremely visual society, there is no limit to what a person can view at the click of a mouse or the buttons on a smartphone. Once the natural eye sees an image, it then creates an image on the heart. Objectionable images can work to kill that Word-seed that has been planted within our hearts. 2 Peter 2:14 refers to having eyes *full of adultery*. What a sobering truth.

On the other hand, in this day of technology, it's easy to download a Bible app on your phone or computer. With it, you are equipped with a concordance, study notes, Bible studies and even a daily verse. We have all this at our fingertips.

If the eyes can be full of adultery, it stands to reason that they can also be full of the good things of God. It all comes down to making choices. We can make the choice to develop our spiritual eyes.

Ears That Hear the Word

The Bible has much to say about our ears and our hearing. Anyone with children can tell you that while children may hear what a parent is saying, they don't always listen. Jesus said as much in this scripture: "...If anyone has ears to hear, let him hear." "Consider carefully what you hear," he continued. "With the measure you use, it will be measured to you – and even more. Whoever has will be given more; whoever does not have, even what he has will be taken from him" (Mark 4:23-25).

We are to take care what we listen to and how we listen. "Having ears, you do not hear," He said to the disciples (Mark 8:18). It's so easy to sit through a church service where a stirring message is being shared, and yet our minds wander and we barely catch the substance of the sermon. But we are responsible for what we have heard. Hearing is essential because, as Apostle Paul points out in Romans 10:17, this is how our faith comes.

Faith will grow when we continually water the seed. Stopping is not an option. Why is it that we give up in a certain area about which we are praying? Because the answer takes too long; we grow weary. We stop watering the seed because we stop hearing the Word. If you are going to stand on God's Word, you stand and stand and keep on standing until you see the manifestation of what you believe.

We must make wise decisions as to what we will allow to enter our spirits by hearing or by not hearing. The choice is ours to make.

The Power of the Tongue

Proverbs 6:2 says we can be *snared* (trapped) by the words that we speak. Jesus made it even clearer when He said, "for by your words you will be acquitted, and by your words you will be condemned" (Matthew 12:37). When we speak, our mind will follow; then actions will follow the mind. We pray for God to provide, but then in the next breath we speak doubt and unbelief. The planted Word can be choked out by unbelief.

When I am not feeling well, I refuse to concentrate on my malady, choosing rather to meditate on the healing scriptures that I know will change my situation. If I am asked how I feel, I remember that God's Word does not hinge on how I feel. God's Word is the final authority in my situation.

At first when you begin to practice speaking the Word over your situation, it may seem as though you are faking. What you are actually doing is agreeing with what God has already ordained. What we say and what we believe about what we say is clarified in Mark 11. "Have faith in God," Jesus answered. "I tell you the truth, if anyone says to this mountain, 'Go, throw yourself into the sea,' and does not doubt in his heart but believes that what he says will happen, it will be done for him. Therefore I tell you, whatever you ask for in prayer, believe that you have received it, and it will be yours" (Mark 11:23, 24).

As you can see, God provides us with a number of ways to nurture the seed of the Word that is planted in our hearts. Once we know how to plant and water, eventually we will see a harvest, which, as it says in Mark 4:8, can be thirty, sixty, or even a hundred times. In Chapter 9 we'll take a closer look at the harvesting and reaping time.

CHAPTER 9
Harvest

In the late spring and early summer, my gardening friends fill baskets with ripe tomatoes, bright yellow squash, tiny potatoes, ears of corn and peppers hot and mild. The taste of these homegrown juicy tender vegetables makes us wonder how some of the produce we buy in stores is even related. The harvest is worth the hard work of planting and tending the garden.

I love getting maximum results in my life. I'm thankful that the Kingdom of God is designed to give us supreme results. Sowing and reaping an abundant harvest is His plan for our lives. "Others, like seed sown on good soil, hear the word, accept it, and produce a crop – thirty, sixty or even a hundred times what was sown" (Mark 4:20).

In this chapter we will see exactly how to become that good soil and how a hundred-time harvest can be a reality in our lives.

The Kingdom of God is run God's way. He says, "This is how my kingdom operates. You put a seed in the ground, and when the seed is properly nourished and cared for, that seed will grow. And when it's time to harvest, put the sickle in and harvest your crop."

This principle is further clarified in this parable: He also said, "This is what the kingdom of God is like. A man scatters seed on the ground. Night and day, whether he sleeps or gets up, the seed sprouts and grows, though he does not know how. All by itself the soil produces grain – first the stalk, then the head, then the full kernel in the head. As soon as the grain is ripe, he puts the sickle to it, because the harvest has come" (Mark 4:26-29).

How the Seed Grows

This parable proves it's not our job to *make our seeds* grow. We pray, we believe and we stand on God's Word, but we cannot make the answer to the prayer come to pass.

If I need a car and I've prayed and I believe God for a car, and then I call my friends to drop hints that I need a car, it becomes manipulation and not faith. We've all been guilty of falling into this trap. We're not quite totally sure that God can come through for us, so we step in and take over. Essentially, we try to answer our own prayers.

There is a difference between putting action to your faith and trying to accomplish what only God can do. We can never make a seed grow. No matter how advanced science becomes – creating hybrids and new strains – they will never be able to make a seed grow. Only God can make the seed grow.

We have seen the importance of cleared ground, prepared soil and planted seed well watered. It's now time to rest in the Lord and believe that he will take care of the rest. If you continue to water the seed with the Word of God, God will be busy night and day causing your seed to mature.

Expectancy

In the first two chapters of this book, we saw how both negative and positive expectancy affect the occurrence of miracles. The principle of expectancy is also echoed in the parable. As soon as the harvest was ready, the farmer was there with his sickle in hand prepared to reap his crop. The KJV says *immediately* he puts in the sickle. This farmer was ready. He had been watching. He was fully confident that his harvest day was coming. He wasn't at his neighbor's house grumbling about the terrible weather. He was attentive to his imminent harvest.

When we pray according to God's Word and according to His promises, His Word *will* come to pass. The principle of seed-time and harvest isn't a "hope so" principle. It always works. Every time we apply God's Word correctly, it will come to pass. Every time.

Mark wrote what happened following Jesus telling the Parable of the Sower.

> That day when evening came, he said to his disciples, "Let us go over to the other side." Leaving the crowd behind, they took him along, just as he was, in the boat. There were also other boats with him. A furious squall came up, and the waves broke over the boat, so that it was nearly swamped. Jesus was in the stern, sleeping on a cushion. The disciples woke him and said to him, "Teacher, don't you care if we drown?"
>
> He got up, rebuked the wind and said to the waves, "Quiet! Be still!" Then the wind died down and it was completely calm.
>
> He said to his disciples, "Why are you so afraid? Do you still have no faith?"

They were terrified and asked each other, "Who is this? Even the wind and the waves obey him!" (Mark 4:35-41)

I can remember puzzling over this passage as to why Jesus came down on them so hard about having no faith. After more study it became clear to me. Jesus specifically told the disciples that they were going to the other side. His point was not to belittle them for their lack of faith, but rather to point out that when His Word went forth, it would surely come to pass – without fail. He wanted them to trust His Word.

This story bolsters my faith. It helps me to know that when I get a Word from God, I can take it to the bank. It's a sure thing. When I sow the seeds of God's Word, I know there will be a harvest. The waves were about to smash the boat, but Jesus had clearly said they were going to the other side. No storm could stop them.

I'd like to take this story one step further. I believe that because of the law of sowing and reaping, Jesus had equipped them to still the storm themselves. He was hoping they would know that He had given them everything they needed to get out of the storm. But fear ruled instead and they couldn't grasp the truth.

If they had put their faith in what He had just taught them, they could have stood up to that storm. They could have yelled out, "Jesus said we are going to the other side, so be still, storm." This story would have ended much differently. Jesus would have awakened as they docked on the other side of the lake. At that point He could have said to them, "Great job, guys. Your faith was tested. You passed because you understood my teaching."

When you make the choice to hold fast to the promises of God, you too will get what Jesus teaches all of us. Your harvest will come when you make this choice. Troubles may occur. Adversities may hurt. Persecutions may come. Life may seem hopeless. But none of these difficulties are greater than God's. When this truth settles in our spirits, we'll have so many harvests, we won't know where to put the sickle first.

Head Faith or Heart Faith?

The disciples heard Jesus say that they were going to the other side; however, the power of that truth wasn't settled deep in their hearts. It was what we call head faith. How can we distinguish head faith from heart faith?

You may hear a message, or read in God's Word that He is greater than all your circumstances; His Name is the highest authority. Then you receive bad news such as learning that you've lost your job. If your initial reaction is, "Oh, no. What am I going to do? We've just bought this new vehicle. We're finished. Bad times are here for sure."

This is head faith, which gives in to unbelief when faced with adversity. Your reaction is based on your mind, will and emotions. To grow your faith, move out of the whine and cry mode and transfer over to speaking the Word, believing the Word, standing on the Word, and trusting the Word. As you do, your faith will grow ever stronger, and you will see the harvest.

Speaking God's Language

If you are honest enough to admit that you are weak in your belief system, begin to laser-focus on God's Word. Jesus has done all the work for us, and we are standing on His shoulders. We are now speaking His language.

I was once in a French speaking country and no one spoke English. All I could hear was noise and I couldn't understand one word. Then in the train station, above the noise I heard a voice speaking English. It came through clear as a bell. I was so happy. I searched for the person who spoke my language.

God understands all the languages on the earth, but he is moved by one language – the language of faith.

Jesus was moved by the tears of Mary as she washed His feet (Luke 7:37, 38), and Jesus himself wept at the grave of Lazarus. It is possible that we are applying our faith through our tears. However, more often than not, our tears are not tears of repentance or even grief, but rather tears of self-pity, fear and unbelief.

After every miracle in the New Testament, Jesus clearly pointed out that the miracle was due to faith.

Activated faith speaks God's language.

Learning Who He Was

In Luke 2, we read about the boy Jesus sitting with the learned men of the day asking many questions. He had stayed behind in Jerusalem, and his parents – in the midst of a large caravan – didn't realize at first that he was missing from the group. When they went back after three days *they found him in the temple courts, sitting among the teachers, listening to them and asking them questions.* (v. 46)

On this day when His parents finally found Him, he was already at work doing the Father's bidding. It was stated clearly in Isaiah 61:

> *The Spirit of the Sovereign Lord is on me, because the Lord has anointed me to proclaim good news to the poor. He has sent me to bind up the brokenhearted, to proclaim freedom for the captives and release from darkness for the prisoners, to proclaim the year of the Lord's favor and the day of vengeance of our God, to comfort all who mourn, and provide for those who grieve in Zion – to bestow on them a crown of beauty instead of ashes, the oil of joy instead of mourning, and a garment of praise instead of a spirit of despair. They will be called oaks of righteousness, a planting of the Lord for the display of his splendor.* (Isaiah 61:1-3)

As a child, Jesus would have sat in the temple hearing the Scriptures. The Word of God prophesied His coming, His power and the miracles he would do.

The question for each one of us is this: Do we see ourselves in the Word? It's all there. This is where we learn who we are in God.

If I had been born into a family of superheroes, I would want to know all about my powers. I would want to know how they came to be; I would want to know their full extent. When we are born again, we have come into a family that is much greater that any fictional superhero.

When we read Isaiah 61, we can put our names in this promise: *I am anointed to preach the good news to the poor... Because Jesus abides in my heart, this scripture is talking about me!* Jesus didn't doubt this promise for a moment and neither should we.

It comes down to choices. Will you believe God's promises and what He says about you or not? I cannot convince you that this scripture is talking about you; it's a realization you must come to on your own. "This day I call heaven and earth as witnesses against you that I have set before you life and death, blessings and curses. Now choose life, so that you and your children may live" (Deuteronomy 30:19).

When my mom chose to hold on to Isaiah 40:31 and to believe that her asthmatic son would one day *run and not grow weary*, it changed my life forever. She planted the seed, nurtured the seed, and watered the seed for years. But one day her harvest came in just as she always believed it would.

Harvest Killers

Two enemies work to kill the harvest – fear and disobedience.

Fear

Fear can strangle faith. You cannot dwell on what you fear and still experience growing faith. Fear indicates that you are not fully trusting God to take care of the situation. Fear grows and becomes more entrenched when it receives the greater attention.

"There is no fear in love. But perfect love drives out fear, because fear has to do with punishment. The one who fears is not made perfect in love" (1 John 4:18). The perfect love mentioned here is not our human love, but the love of God that we allow to fill our hearts. If His love is designed to drive out fear, then fear must not be a part of our language.

Disobedience

The other harvest-killer is disobedience. The more you study God's Word, the more you know God's Word, the more responsible you are for the knowledge you have. James 4:17 says that if we know to do something and fail to do it, we are sinning.

For example, when you have a sharp disagreement with a friend, and then you hear a message or you read in the Word, about the importance of forgiveness, you must forgive. But if you aren't willing to humble yourself and forgive, you have compromised the harvest of the Word. The Word was planted, but it has now been choked out. To protect the harvest of manifested miracles, we must constantly double check that we haven't stepped over into disobedience.

Earlier we saw the response of the young ruler (Luke 18). He walked away from Jesus. He stepped into disobedience and subsequently lost his harvest. I have no doubt – according to God's Word – that if he had sold his riches he would have ended up with ten times as much. This was a smart man. He was a ruler, a leader. God could have used him in the most incredible way, but he failed to see past the present moment. He couldn't trust God. His disobedience caused him to go away sadly with no harvest.

The God of the Harvest is a Big God

Many of us have heard the wrong teaching. We've been taught about a small God, an arbitrary God, a changeable God. That mindset is mistaken. When we renew our minds by the Word, we are promised that we will then know God's perfect will (Romans 12:2). What an extraordinary promise – to know God's perfect will.

We must renew our mind beyond what other people say, beyond the bad news that comes though the media. What does God say about the situation? What does God say about each one of us? We should be making faith statements like the following:

I am God's anointed.

I am His child.

I am blessed of the Lord.

I am the head and not the tail.

I dwell in the secret place of the most high God.

I will trust and not be afraid…

Create your own list. Keep your list before you. Let your ears and your mind hear your voice speak these words aloud.

However big you think God is, He's bigger. However far you think you can trust Him, by His grace you can trust Him further. However much you think He can do in your life, He will do exceedingly, abundantly beyond what words can even describe.

In our next and final chapter, we'll talk about perseverance and how it's possible to maintain a level of faith so that we don't cave in when the going gets rough.

CHAPTER 10
Perseverance

We are not brought into the Kingdom of God simply to get a ticket to heaven, although that is an awesome gift and privilege. We are brought into the Kingdom to be more than conquerors and to have victory against our adversary, the devil. We are light in a very dark world. We are designed to be world-changers for God. "Therefore put on the full armor of God, so that when the day of evil comes, you may be able to stand your ground, and after you have done everything, to stand" (Ephesians 6:13).

Why then are many Christians weak and ineffective? I could probably list several reasons, but close to the top of that list would be the inability to persevere. You've heard the old saying, "When the going gets tough, the tough get going." For many Christians, when the going gets tough, they give up and quit.

In the above verse from Ephesians, we are encouraged to be totally decked out in the armor of God – He provides each piece of armor for us – and to stand our ground using our weapon, which is the Word of God. When you have done everything you know to do and you still don't see the manifestation of the miracle you need, keep on standing. Don't move. Keep standing. Perseverance of this kind will change you, change your situation and change the world around you.

Unfortunately, we don't persevere. We read God's Word and we make a decision to believe it, but when our situation doesn't turn out like we thought or wished we give up. Though we have applied faith and prayer, we lose hope.

Turn the Other Cheek

When I was a kid, I learned about turning the other cheek as advised in Luke 6:29. But no one taught us what to do after we had turned the other cheek. There was a bully in our primary school who hit me constantly. One day David, the bully, hit me in the face.

I said, "That's no problem, here's my other cheek." He most willingly hit me again. I didn't know what to do after that. It didn't turn out as I had planned. I thought when I "turned my other cheek" his heart would soften and he would become my friend. Instead all I got was another smack.

But that's not the end of the story. I didn't give up on David. Soon after that I invited him to church and later watched as he gave his heart to Jesus. When I received the second smack, it seemed I lost that skirmish. But in the overall war, God's Word prevailed.

The life of faith is impossible to live if you don't realize that the righteous man falls down seven times, but he gets up again (Proverbs 24:16). It's the getting up again part that will move you forward in your faith journey.

When Things Don't Turn Out as Expected

In Judges 20, we find a fascinating event where the results were not expected. It takes place during a sad time in Israel's history when the tribes of Israel were involved in a civil war.

Several men from Gibeah, a town in the region of Benjamin, had committed an atrocity. The other tribes asked that the wrongdoers be turned over "so that we may put them to death and purge the evil from Israel" (Judges 20:13). The Benjamites refused to give up the lawbreakers and war was on.

At once the Benjamites mobilized twenty-six thousand swordsmen from their towns, in addition to seven hundred chosen men from those living in Gibeah. Among all these soldiers there were seven hundred chosen men who were left-handed, each of whom could sling a stone at a hair and not miss.

Israel, except for the tribe of Benjamin, mustered four hundred thousand swordsmen, all of them fighting men.

The Israelites went up to Bethel and inquired of God. They said, "Who of us shall go first to fight against the Benjamites?"

The Lord replied, "Judah shall go first."

The next morning the Israelites got up and pitched camp near Gibeah. The men of Israel went out to fight the Benjamites and took up battle positions against them at Gibeah. The Benjamites came out of Gibeah and cut down twenty-two thousand Israelites on the battlefield that day. But the men of Israel encouraged one another and again took up their positions where they had stationed themselves the first day. (Judges 20:15-22)

The battle didn't turn out as the Israelites expected. They prayed, connected with God and went into battle. They got mowed down, which was discouraging and devastating.

Yet their response was to encourage one another and pray again:

The Israelites went up and wept before the Lord until evening, and they inquired of the Lord. They said, "Shall we go up again to battle against the Benjamites, our brothers?"

The Lord answered, "Go up against them."

Then the Israelites drew near to Benjamin the second day. This time, when the Benjamites came out from Gibeah to oppose them, they cut down another eighteen thousand Israelites, all of them armed with swords.

Then the Israelites, all the people, went up to Bethel, and there they sat weeping before the Lord. They fasted that day until evening and presented burnt offerings and fellowship offerings to the Lord. (Judges 20:23-26)

Once again the Israelites were defeated. It seemed as if God had gone deaf. The battle-ready veterans of war were reduced to weeping. Their discouragement was deep and profound. Even though they prayed and fasted, nothing was going right at all. They'd witnessed the slaughter of tens of thousands of their best fighting men. I'm sure they thought it was time to turn tail and run.

You and I have faced such circumstances. We seem to be doing everything according to what we know to do. Yet we see no improvement in our situation. In fact, things seems to be going from bad to worse. *We feel as if we should give up.* This faith stuff is not working. It may work for others but it's not working for me.

Instead of quitting, remember the Ephesians verse. After you have done everything, stand. When there seems to be no other course to take, persist. Hold firm. Believing God's Word is not an on-again, off-again undertaking. To see the miracles, stand on God's promises, and keep standing. And then keep standing again.

Not a Matter of Pick-and-Choose

I told you about how a verse in Joel encouraged and helped my mom when I was a child. The verse proclaims that the Lord will restore the years that the locusts have destroyed (Joel 2:25).

Those locusts had come into our family in swarms. It seemed to be utterly impossible that any good could come out of the abuse that my mom suffered and the way our family broke apart.

But God is at His best in impossible situations. There was a time in our lives when we had no place to call home. We were homeless. My father had previously kicked us out of the house and now we faced a true dilemma. A single mother, with no college education, two small children to support… and now no home. My uncle insisted that we come stay with him until we got back on our feet. The three of us shared a small room, but we never felt sorry for ourselves because every morning and every night my mom would paint a picture of where God would take us if we trusted in Him. She would tell us about scriptures like Deuteronomy 28:13: "The LORD will make you the head, not the tail…" In the natural it was an absolute impossibility that we could be the head of anything; in the natural we were the tail, but we were dealing with a supernatural God.

One day my brother and I would captain every sports team that we played for, one day God would give us an international business and one day we would own the house where we had shared a bedroom. One day we would go from the family who was in desperate need to a family who was now able to meet the needs of others.

It's not a matter of pick-and-choose regarding the promises of God. Either they are true, or they are not. I choose to believe them all. I believe that the same Jesus who said He was going to prepare a place for me in heaven also said that I would do greater works on this earth than He did. So I keep jumping back into the battle. I don't give up. I clean my wounds. Sometimes I cry and maybe I'll even whine a little. But then I go right back to praying, throwing myself on God's mercy. I read His eternal Word. I don't stop until victory!

Sometimes we feel that our dire circumstances and unendurable pain can never be turned around for good. But God promised that after a night of weeping joy comes in the morning (Psalm 30:5). During our darkest night, we can't imagine joy, but God promises that it will come. So we must continue to stand.

They Saw Their Victory

The Israelite army stood firm. No matter that they had been routed two times in a row. They continued to trust in their God.

And the Israelites inquired of the Lord. (In those days the ark of the covenant of God was there, with Phinehas son of Eleazar, the son of Aaron, ministering before it). They asked, "Shall we go up again to battle with Benjamin our brother, or not?"

The Lord responded, "Go, for tomorrow I will give them into your hands."

Then Israel set an ambush around Gibeah. They went up against the Benjamites on the third day and took up positions against Gibeah as they had done before. The Benjamites came out to meet them and were drawn away from the city. They began to inflict casualties on the Israelites as before, so that about thirty men fell in the open field and on the roads – the one leading to Bethel and the other to Gibeah.

While the Benjamites were saying, "We are defeating them as before," the Israelites were saying, "Let's retreat and draw them away from the city to the roads."

All the men of Israel moved from their places and took up positions at Baal Tamar, and the Israelite ambush charged out of its place on the west of Gibeah. Then ten thousand of Israel's finest men made a frontal attack on Gibeah. The fighting was so heavy that the Benjamites did not realize how near disaster was. The Lord defeated Benjamin before Israel, and on that day the Israelites struck down 25,100 Benjamites, all armed with swords. Then the Benjamites saw that they were beaten. (Judges 20:27-36)

At last, the Israelites saw victory. The person who refuses to give up can never be defeated. The person who refuses to quit can never lose. A battle mentality helps us to refuse to back off – the kind of tenacity we saw in the paralyzed man at the Pool of Bethesda. His hopes for healing seemed impossible, but he never gave up. After thirty-eight years of waiting, most people would quit. But he didn't quit. The healing day finally came when Jesus walked by.

We meet failure and all seems hopeless but we don't see answers right around the corner.

Have you ever given up on praying for a miracle? What was the reason? Most often it is because we don't see *results*. We prayed. We believed. Nothing happened. God never promised that your miracle would come immediately. Your answered prayer may be immediate or it may take years.

Will I Find Faith?

Once, Jesus explained how important it is to pray and not give up.

He said: *"In a certain town there was a judge who neither feared God nor cared about men. And there was a widow in that town who kept coming to him with the plea, 'Grant me justice against my adversary.'*

"For some time he refused. But finally he said to himself, 'Even though I don't fear God or care about men, yet because this widow keeps bothering me, I will see that she gets justice, so that she won't eventually wear me out with her coming!'"

And the Lord said, "Listen to what the unjust judge says. And will not God bring about justice for his chosen ones, who cry out to him day and night? Will he keep putting them off? I tell you, he will see that they get justice, and quickly. However, when the Son of Man comes, will he find faith on the earth?" (Luke 18:2-8)

Notice that Jesus finishes this parable by asking the question, "Will I find faith?" He didn't say,

- Will I find people attending church?
- Will I find people who know all the words to the praise songs?
- Will I find people who believe I exist?

No, His question was, "Will I find faith?" When Jesus returns and examines my heart, when He looks at my life, will He find me full of faith and constant expectancy? Will He say, "Well done good and faithful servant" as He did to the servant in the Parable of the Talents?

Those who are full of faith are constantly pushing the boundaries, constantly stretching their faith. They are not afraid to believe for miracles. They are ready to pray for others and then believe God for the answers.

It's strange, but true, that a person can live a Christian life without exercising a great deal of faith. Everything is comfortable, everything is within reach, there's no cause to trust God on a daily basis. It becomes a life of complacency in the spiritual realm.

Instead of complacency and self-satisfaction, trust God. If all is well with you, then find someone who is struggling financially who you can stand and believe with. Ask God to show you ways in which you can expand your sphere of influence. Who needs your friendship? Who needs your faith to join with theirs in order to see an amazing move of God? Never allow status quo or self-righteousness to make your faith weak.

A Dangerous Situation

We conducted a mission trip to South Africa with a thirty-person team from Aspen, Colorado. During the trip, we went to a township hospital to pray for the sick. We were told we were crazy because so many patients had contagious diseases and were dying; it would be too dangerous. We went to the hospital anyway.

We didn't go for a photo opportunity nor were we there for glory. We wanted to stand on God's Word and pray. We wanted to bring light into a very dark place.

We prayed with little children who were in ICU and had only a short time to live. Later, we returned and some of those children were no longer in the hospital – not because they died, but because they recovered.

God's Word promises that if we lay hands on the sick they will recover (Mark 16:18).

I'm sure you wonder about those who don't recover. When you get brave enough to lay hands on the sick and nothing happens, what then?

The answer is: You do it again. And again. And again. You continue to go back into battle. When you feel you may have lost the battle, it's time to get on your knees and pray and seek fresh direction and a fresh anointing. But never stop. Never give up.

The more you persevere, the more your faith grows. The more faith grows the more you use it exactly as Jesus illustrated in the Parable of the Talents (Chapter 5). Two servants quickly stepped out, trusted their master and doubled their money. They used their faith and reaped the harvest.

God's Strength or Our Strength?

When we engage in faith battles, we do not fight in our own strength or even with our own equipment. Our armor is given to us by God (Ephesians 6:10-18). We will fight effectively in His armor.

But if we stop trusting in God and move into our own strength, we will not win the battles. How do we know when we have shed God's armor and put on our own? When we begin to be weary, our reasoning and strength brings tiredness and burnout.

When you feel exhausted, weak, fatigued and tired, it is time to double check your power source and your armor. God's strength never fails, never gives up and does not grow weary. Trusting in His Word and in His character, you will find the energy to remain consistent in the faith.

Persistent Faith

I have seen the miraculous results of persistent faith in numerous ways in my life, but one that is especially close to my heart and is especially meaningful to me has to do with my father.

My father was an extremely angry and abusive man. I still see scenes in my head of him physically hurting my mother. Eventually, as mentioned above, he simply kicked us out of the house – my mother, my brother, and me – leaving us with nothing. While my mother had every right to be bitter and vindictive, she wasn't. All through my growing up years, she said nothing negative about my father, nor would she allow Clint or I to speak disparagingly of him. She even made us call him every Father's Day and on his birthday, although we never wanted to. She would simply say, "He's your father. And it honor's God." We constantly prayed for him to give his life to Jesus.

Fast forward to Aspen, Colorado when Clint and I became members of a small, struggling church. It was in my heart to begin a Sunday evening Bible study to help the church grow and to help people grow in their faith. I was too naïve to realize that jealousy exists in the church. The Sunday night Bible study audience grew quickly but Sunday morning attendance remained the same.

The result was that we were asked to leave the church. We had been so excited because we saw God change lives and suddenly out of nowhere, the church leadership told us to leave. We were shocked and very discouraged. I'd never been kicked out of a church before. I can't describe how horrible it made me feel.

We were doing what we thought was right (like those Israelites in Judges 20) and yet we were mowed down. During that time of discouragement, at one of the lowest points in my life, I decided to create a video that I called, "How to Come to Jesus." Though I was hurt and felt defeated, I continued to do what I believed God had called me to do, and that is speak His Word and tell others about His goodness and mercy.

Years later when my father died, I asked God to please give me a sign about my father's eternity. I was desperate to know because I had prayed for my father for so many years. The thought came (I know the thought came from God) to look on my father's computer. There I saw the date that my own father viewed the video I had made years before. He had viewed it only a short time before he died and had committed his life to Christ.

At that moment I had a deep settled peace that my father had indeed been saved and that I would meet him one day in heaven. My mother's years of consistent prayers were not in vain. And my seed that I sowed in a time of intense pain allowed me to reap in joy.

This is only one example – I could cite many more – that proves to me that perseverance in our lives, in our faith and in standing on the Word will result in seeing incredible miracles come to pass.

After you have done *everything*, stand. And then keep on standing.

If you want to experience God's miracles in your life, that's the only way!

Conclusion

Throughout the journey of this book, a number of steps have been presented to help make it crystal clear that ongoing miracles are part and parcel of God's plan for the lives of His children. In Judges 6 when the young man named Gideon was approached by the Angel of the Lord, he cried out, *Where are all his wonders or miracles that our fathers told us about?*

Today, the majority of Christians are unaware of the possibility of miracles and lack the understanding to even utter such a cry as Gideon. Become a person who cries out, "Where are Your miracles Lord? Show us Your miracles."

Then begin to expect to experience His miracles as was pointed out in the first part of the book. Here's a quick review of how to use the principles of seed-time and harvest in order to see miracles manifest.

Bad Weather

Those who don't know God, don't trust His Word and don't believe His promises will see very few miracles in their lives because of their negative expectancy. Unbelief prevented Jesus from performing miracles in His own hometown. Is doubt and unbelief hindering miracles in your life?

Sunshine and Rain

We must learn to positively expect miracles. We saw how the strong positive expectancy of Jairus, the distraught father, and the woman with the issue of blood, drove them to action. Their positive expectancy resulted in manifested miracles. We can do the same thing every day as we look to our God and expect Him to bring miracles.

Blight

Do you see suffering in life as something an angry God is doing to you? You may have confused who your real enemy is. The devil comes to kill, steal, and destroy (John 10:10). God has designed a way for you to be victorious through *every* trial. With Jesus as our example, we too can begin to see suffering as a stepping-stone to a higher level in our life of victory.

Love in the Garden

Our faith works by love (Galatians 5:6). God's love for you activates your faith. When you are resting in His love, when you are confident of His love, then you can know your prayers will be answered. You will no longer be hesitant to reach out and pray for others. When they experience miracles, they will be introduced to God' unconditional love, too.

Where to Plant

Positioning is another way to open the doors to miracles. Consistently place yourself where God is. Where is God the most accessible? It might be in your regular quiet prayer time in your own home, or joining with other believers in regular church services. You can position your heart and mind by continually expecting God to move in a miraculous way. He draws near to those who draw near to Him (James 4:8).

Seed

Seed-time and harvest is a heavenly principle that is demonstrated in the earth. It's as binding as the law of gravity. The seed is the Word of God. In Matthew 4:4 Jesus clearly states, *"Man does not live on bread alone, but on every word that comes from the mouth of God."* The seed of the Word is essential for you to experience miracles in your life.

You sow into your own life the Word of God. If your pastor is the only sower of the Word in your life, you are in a lot of trouble because you only spend a small portion of your time in church. If you sow no seeds during the week, then there will be a low chance that you will experience miracles. Period.

Soil

In order for the seed of the Word to grow, the land must be cleared. Clear your soil from these four hindrances.

Rocks: Rocks are obstacles such as envy and selfish ambition.

Weeds: Weeds are disrupters–the cares, anxieties, and distractions of life.

Roots: Roots are little prejudices, behavior issues and pet peeves (what gets on our nerves) that we let slide by. We don't pay attention and these small issues turn into roots.

Trees: Trees are good but unnecessary parts of life. Never let trees take over the garden. Move trees to the periphery.

Planting and Watering

Constantly infuse the Word into your mind. Satan, who prowls around looking for whomever he can devour (1 Peter 5:8), comes to steal the Word, because he doesn't want it to take root and grow in your life. If you believe the Word is the final authority, then you will obey the Word and you will experience manifested miracles.

Harvest

When you pray according to God's Word and according to His promises, your harvest will come. Troubles may surface, adversities may appear and persecutions may come. You may feel you are finished, but no problem, danger, difficulty or harassment is greater than God's promises. When this truth is settled in your spirit, you will have so many harvests; you won't know where to put in the sickle first.

Perseverance

Your circumstances may convince you that there is no hope and no chance for good. Yet God promised that after a night of weeping joy comes in the morning (Psalm 30:5). During the dark night you can't imagine joy ever coming but God promises that it will. So choose to stand.

It's not a matter of pick-and-choose regarding the promises of God. Either they are true or they are not. I choose to believe them all.

***

Make a choice and start today to put these seed-time and harvest principles into action. When you do, your life will never be the same – I can assure you. Your life will be revolutionized and the ripple effect will go out to every person with whom you come in contact.

God is looking for someone to be salt and light. Could it be you?

"For the eyes of the LORD run to and fro throughout the whole earth, to shew himself strong in the behalf of them whose heart is perfect toward him" (2 Chronicles 16:9 KJV).

The Greatest Miracle

Without a doubt raising the dead has to be the greatest miracle. There is one last question that I want to ask you before you put this book down. Is Jesus Christ the Lord and Savior of your life? I am not asking whether or not you attend church nor am I asking if you belong to a denomination. Have you experienced the resurrecting power of Jesus in your life? Have you experienced the hope that breaks through the darkness? If not, your greatest miracle is about to happen to you right now.

The Bible says "Everyone who calls on the name of the Lord will be saved" (Romans 10:17.) Are you part of that "Everyone"? If so, then the rest of the verse applies to you, too. Right now, where you are, call upon the name of Jesus and in your own words ask Him to forgive you, to save you, to make you brand new. Jesus died and rose again so that you can have life and life overflowing. A miracle to your body is pale in comparison to complete healing in your soul. A financial miracle is minuscule in comparison to the healing of your heart. Jesus wants to revive and renew every aspect of your life, if you will let Him. Today is the day of your salvation (2 Corinthians 6:2).

God bless you precious friend.

---

http://www.biblegateway.com/blog/2012/02/how-can-you-meditate-on-gods-word/

Testimonies of God's Miracles

Tammy's Story

When I was a young girl, my younger brother, Timothy, was two years old and a very curious, playful little guy. One Saturday morning while we kids were watching cartoons, my mom was busy in the kitchen and Dad on the phone to a friend. Unbeknownst to anyone, Tim had gone outside on his own.

Suddenly my mom saw him from the kitchen window and screamed! Dad looked up from his phone call and saw Tim floating face down in the swimming pool.

My mother ran outside and jumped into the swimming pool with her dressing gown on and pulled Tim from the water. His face was blue and he was not breathing. He was completely limp. My mother was beside herself. As she lay Tim down on the floor, Dad told us all to pray! My father's voice echoed out over the neighborhood as he called out the name of Jesus over and over again. He didn't stop praying! A family friend, who lived down the road, heard the commotion and came running. Miraculously, she had just completed first-aid course and she gave Timothy mouth to mouth resuscitation. Meanwhile we continued to pray, calling on God to spare our brother. At last, he started to breathe just as the ambulance arrived. They rushed him off to the hospital. The doctors who treated Tim said it was a miracle that he was alive but we were warned that he would have brain damage. Today, I can happily report that there is absolutely nothing physically wrong with Tim. He is completely healthy and strong and is studying to become a lawyer. How thankful I am for a father who believed in the power of prayer, and who believed in a God who hears and answers prayers!

Duncan's Story

During my childhood, my father was a career officer in the Air Force which meant we moved about every three to four years. This meant new environments and new friends were a common part of my growing-up years. Another common part of my childhood was health issues. I was born with two health problems that, while they were not life threatening, certainly gave cause for concern. One of these was a back defect. In my infant years, a portion of one of my vertebrae did not fully develop. To look at it in an X-ray, it looked as if a bite was taken out the vertebrae. Although it couldn't be seen outwardly, it had a dramatic impact on my life. As a child, I had to be careful about anything that could put strain on the lower back. As I grew, I began to have back pain and the doctors were concerned that I might have a curvature of the spine.

By age eleven, I was wearing a back brace that looked like a corset worn by women in the 1800's.

Every morning, I wrapped this contraption around me and string it up nice and tight. I would go under my clothes, but it was pretty obvious the girdle was there. You can imagine the teasing that took place.

At times when I sat down my back would "lock up" and I was unable to get up without assistance. Other times, I would lower my head, and due to the pinched nerves, pain would shoot down my back. At times the pain was so severe I passed out.

My parents were told that I would not grow much more than 5'8". That wouldn't be so bad, but I came from a family of tall people. My dad was 6'2" and my mother was 5'11". Before I reached my teens I already wore size 13 shoe, which meant I looked like a big "L" with no prospects of my body catching up to my feet!

My mother was a great woman of faith and she was a prayer warrior. My dad, although a believer, was not vocal about his faith. However, one day Dad had had enough. He'd just received the doctor's report that I would never grow past 5'8". He began to take authority and cry out to the Lord, asking Him to heal me.

Things did not change immediately, but in the summer between my sophomore and junior years I grew *eight full inches*. I shot up from 5'8" to 6'4" in just 3 months. My body was producing calcium so fast, it filled in the missing bone in my lower back. Then as a freshman in college I grew an additional 2". Today, at age 54, I rarely have back problems and I live a full, productive, healthy life.

The scripture says that "the prayers of a righteous man avail much."

(James 5:16) I thank God daily for my healing and for parents who cried out to the Lord on behalf of their children.

Stephanie's Story

I grew up in South Africa speaking only English, even though my parents were German. At the age of thirteen I moved to Germany with my mom. Not being able to speak a word and barely understanding the language did not make things easy! A month after we arrived I started attending a regular school – still not able to speak or understand the language. We had to translate my homework from German into English, so that I could understand it. We would then do it in English and translate it back into German! It was a nightmare. This went on for a time through struggles, tears, and tons of questions! But my mother continued to pray and told me, "Trust God! With Him you CAN do this!" I'm so thankful that we serve an almighty, all-powerful God! After about six months I was able to read and write the language. Two years after that I finished tenth grade the second best in my class. Now I am getting my degree at a German university!

Glory to God. He is the God of the impossible!

Kim's Story

I had a miraculous event where God used me to demonstrate to several non-believers that He is alive and active in the world today. When I worked in recruitment, everyone in the office block knew I was a Christian. Some of them accepted it and others mocked me. One man in particular would often ridicule me and make subtle jabs at my faith. For the purpose of this account I'll call him Steve. After work one evening we were in the parking garage and the electric gate jammed. This meant no one could drive his or her car out to go home. Next to the gate was a box, which allowed the gate to be opened manually in case of an emergency. That particular evening the man who had the key to the box was not there. I went inside to call someone to come get me. It would be no problem to just leave my car at work. However, there was no answer at the house.

There were about five or of us standing at the gate, including Steve. I clearly heard God speak to my spirit and tell me to lay hands on the gate and pray for it. I was constantly asking God to show Himself to my colleagues and now He was answering my prayer.

At first I didn't listen; I went back inside to call home again, but still no answer. At that point, I went back out to the gate and laid my hands on it and quietly prayed for it to open. This heavy electric gate immediately opened. My colleagues who were standing there asked me how I managed to open the gate. I told them that I prayed and God opened the gate. Most of them were quiet, but Steve just laughed and made a comment about how ridiculous that was. Everyone, except Steve, went back inside and the word about what had happened was soon common knowledge throughout the office block. I was the first to leave and as I drove out the open gate, Steve – who professed to doubt – called to me and said, "Hey you can't leave. What if the gate closes again?" I guess he believed it after all.

I worshiped the Lord the whole way home for His faithfulness and His compassion.

Mike's Story

In January 2009, I was at a perfect place in my life. My family was well, I was well, my business was going strong – I even had money in the bank. The following month, I was in Cape Town, South Africa, where I was working an event (that's what I do – event management) when an accident happened. I fell four stories off of a crane due to the crane driver's error. Nearly everything that could be broken or shattered in my body had been broken and shattered. For instance, my right elbow shattered in 400 places (that's when the surgeon stopped counting).

I lay in ICU, unable to move for 10 days. On the day after the accident I prayed and simply asked the Lord to get me through that day. I realized I had already experienced my first miracle – living through such a traumatic fall. I started undergoing surgeries for my different injuries, which amounted to fourteen by the end of the year. During which time I was on heavy medication which throws a person into unnatural depression. I struggled with intense discouragement. My challenges worsened during this time. My wife had already been experiencing dissatisfaction and loneliness in the marriage and now she wanted out. This series of events was more than she could handle. Of course, my business suffered in my absence. My primary partner had kept it all together as I spent much of my days sleeping and recovering from the surgeries. We took on a new partner but he didn't work out well. At one point we considered shutting it all down and terminating the company. My life appeared to be in failure mode, but I had been taught that God's Word is true, and that it does not return void. My pastor told me, "Failure is not fatal with God."

I wanted my marriage healed and I wanted to be whole, not just physically, but emotionally and spiritually – so I started undergoing personal counseling. My nine months of counseling were not easy. Being immobilized gave me time for personal introspection and spiritual acclimatization. The Holy Spirit had started His work. I witnessed a change within my spirit. At the same time I was dealing with surgeries and rehabilitation, my faith was being stirred and regenerated. My friends got together and began to pray for my marriage. My parents were praying, my in-laws were praying, and soon my wife and I were going through marriage counseling together. We were taught to say to one another: "You are valuable and precious to me" – whether we felt like the words were true or not.

One of my injuries caused a blood clot in my ear, which caused a ringing in the ear that kept me from sleeping. I decided to let those sleepless nights be my prayer time. I walked outside around our property and cried out to God. I can say that many of my character traits have been transformed because of this holy time with God. I knew that a true spiritual awakening needed to happen, and even though physical setbacks were taxing, the ensuing spiritual quest was liberating.

Fast forward to February 2013 – four years later – I've experienced a multitude of miracles. God not only healed our marriage, but He gave us a gift of friendship and companionship few ever experience. We have been blessed with another daughter – yet another miracle. God not only saved our business but also increased it. And He has healed my body – in spite of the negative prognoses from doctors and surgeons. He protected me and cushioned me from a four-story fall. He got me through that first day and all sixteen surgeries in the year and a half to follow. The greatest miracle is this: God can achieve the impossible for you and resurrect all aspects of your life. He did it for me and He will do it for you!

Laurie's Story

From earliest childhood it had always been my dream to get married and raise a family. I met the man of my dreams in 1982 while attending church. It was love at first sight. We met and were engaged in six weeks and married seven months later. When we married I was 27 years old and my husband was 24. We had great jobs, attended an amazing church and had wonderful friends. Everything seemed to be much like that dream that I always believed in. A couple years into our marriage we were ready to have children. This was something that we always wanted and just knew that the time was right. However, month after month we failed to get pregnant. We continued to believe and pray, but for nearly two years it was an ongoing struggle.

I finally went to the doctor to see if possibly there might be a problem. Upon examination we were told that I had fibroid tumors. They were not malignant, and certainly not life threatening, but we were told it was highly unlikely that we would ever get pregnant. As you can imagine I was devastated. The dream I had had as a child now seemed to be impossible. We were sad, sometimes angry, and greatly disappointed.

My husband and I knew Jesus as our Lord and Savior. We knew that the Bible says that "all things work together for good." (Romans 8:28) But it also says, "no good thing will he withhold from those who walk uprightly." (Psalm 84:11) So it was a time of real confusion and doubt for both of us.

Then one Tuesday morning, while getting ready for work, I turned on the television – something I NEVER did. The program that was airing that moment was the 700 Club with Pat Robertson. I was fixing my hair and listening to them praying on the program. All of a sudden Pat made this statement: "I see a young girl out there who has believed for a child for a long time. The Lord hears your cry. He sees your tears, and He is bringing healing to your womb and will give you a child." When I heard that, something inside of me was stirred. I knew that promise was for me.

There was a sense of peace, a knowing and a gratitude that cannot be put into words. I knew God had healed me. In fact, I knew that I was pregnant. I pondered it in my heart for a few days. I planned to wait until Saturday morning to take another in home pregnancy test. My husband had asked me not to buy any more pregnancy tests because of the emotional pain we experienced when they were negative. But this time was different. I KNEW I was pregnant. Saturday morning rolled around. I was waiting for the in-home test results. (This was back in the 80s and it took about fifteen or twenty minutes back then.) When my husband woke up, I told him what had happened. He had not heard the Word I had received so his natural response was, "Now honey, I appreciate the fact that you feel this Word is for you, but let's be careful not to get our hopes up." At that time, because of our *religious* upbringing we believed God *could* do miracles, but didn't always believe that He *would.* Our conservative theology had put God in a box and left no room for Him to be God. This was different. Regardless of what I thought or felt, I believed.

We waited for the 20 or so minutes, and went to look at the in-home test. *It was positive!* We literally fell to our knees in tears and thanked God for healing me! God used the word from a preacher on television to let me know that He had performed a miracle. I scheduled an appointment with my doctor. He confirmed the pregnancy and with tears in his eyes he asked if he could pray and bless this child. Nine months later we had Sarah! Then God proved His healing was complete, when we had our second daughter, Seliece, nineteen months later. We now have three daughters who have brought immeasurable joy and happiness into our lives. They all love and serve the Lord. On April, 2013, we celebrated our 30th Anniversary. We're grateful for the many miracles that the Lord has provided for us over the years.

Thank You!

I pray that you have been greatly encouraged by God's Word and that the time you have spent reading this book has planted seeds in your heart that will bear much fruit in your life. You were made to do great things with God.

                          – Brent

To contact Brent Phillips for your next event:

NeverJustExist
1415 South Voss #110-399
Houston, TX 77057

Phone: 713-367-1859
Email: contact@NeverJustExist.org
Web: www.NeverJustExist.org
Twitter: brentgphillips
Facebook: neverjustexist